"Chris Webb models God's beautiful call to grow as a disciple with our head and our heart, our whole bodies and our whole lives, without division or separation. His writing draws us deeper into rich wells of Christian spirituality with an undefended joy, a radical edge, and an encouraging word. Chris reminds us of the life-changing call to know we are beloved as children in Christ, held alongside the transforming call to grow into all that means in all parts of life every day. This is no microwavable, just add boiling water, spirituality-lite; this goes deeper into the things of eternal life."

Barry Hill, rector of Market Harborough, diocese of Leicester, UK

"With the eye of a poet and the heart of a pastor, Chris Webb cuts through the din and despair of modern society with a call to true discipleship: live in the embrace of a loving God and rejoice, one and all, with your whole being. I can think of no finer encouragement for women and men, and no better word of hope for the communities we share."

Samuel Rahberg, author of *Enduring Ministry*

"With picture-filled prose and deep insights, Chris Webb has done it again. First he illuminated the pages of Scripture with *The Fire of the Word*, and now he has set aglow everyday life with the light of kingdom living. This is a beautifully written and immensely important book about living life with God."

Gary W. Moon, executive director, Martin Institute and Dallas Willard Center, Westmont College

"What a special book of great depth. Drawing deep from biblical and ancient writings, Chris Webb paints an accessible and compelling vision of life today in God's kingdom."

Nathan Foster, director of community life for Renovaré, author of *Wisdom Chaser* and *The Making of an Ordinary Saint*

"Chris Webb is the master of holy mischief and sacred disruption. He subverts our fallacious norms by rooting us deeper in the truths of Scripture and the ways of Jesus. Your heart pounds as you read this book. It pounds because of the beautiful pictures it paints. It pounds because your hunger for an eternity of great significance is exposed. Your heart pounds because as you read Chris grabs hold of your sleeve and enthusiastically pulls you breathlessly toward your soul's sure home. We can live our eternity now, and Chris Webb's *God-Soaked Life* makes clear the Christ path that get us there!"

Eric Leroy Wilson, author of *Faith: The First Seven Lessons*

GOD SOAKED LIFE

Discovering a Kingdom Spirituality

CHRIS WEBB

HODDER &
STOUGHTON

Scripture quotations, unless otherwise noted, are from the New Revised
Standard Version of the Bible, copyright 1989 by the Division of
Christian Education of the National Council of the Churches of Christ
in the USA. Used by permission. All rights reserved.

Published in association with Inter Varsity Press

First published in Great Britain in 2017 by Hodder & Stoughton
An Hachette UK company

I

Copyright © Christopher S. Webb

A CIP catalogue record for this title is available from the British Library

ISBN 978 1 473 66526 2
eBook ISBN 978 1 473 66527 9

Printed and bound in the UK by
Clays Ltd, St Ives plc

Hodder & Stoughton policy is to use papers that are natural,
renewable and recyclable products and made from wood grown in
sustainable forests. The logging and manufacturing processes are expected
to conform to the environmental regulations of the country of origin.

Hodder & Stoughton Ltd
Carmelite House
50 Victoria Embankment
London EC4Y 0DZ

www.hodderfaith.com

FOR SALLY

"Y mae llawer o ferched

wedi gweithio'n fedrus,

ond yr wyt ti'n

rhagori arnynt i gyd."

DIARHEBION 31:29 (BCN)

CONTENTS

Prologue   I

1 THE INVITATION

God-Soaked Creation   7

Broken People   14

God's Delight   21

Over to You   26

2 HEART RENEWAL

A New Heart   31

Love in Everything   36

Soul Healing   43

Over to You   50

3 FEARLESS HONESTY

The Truth Deep Within   55

Play-Actors   62

Confessions   69

Over to You   75

4 CLOSE TO THE FATHER'S HEART

Longing of the Heart   79

Intimacy and Separation   87

The Journey into God   93

Over to You   101

5   GOD IN EVERYDAY LIFE

God in All Things   105

Learning to See   110

Learning Attentiveness   117

Over to You   124

6   CREATING COMMUNITY

Love Without Borders   129

The Great Commission   136

Learning Love in Gentleness   142

Over to You   150

7   THE POLITICS OF LOVE

Against the Darkness   155

Glorious Possibilities   161

The Kingdom Today   170

Over to You   176

Epilogue   179

Taking Part   183

Acknowledgments   185

Notes   189

PROLOGUE

IMAGINE THE DAY AFTER YOUR DEATH.

You find yourself waking up to a new and glorious reality. This place—what shall we call it? Heaven? Eternity? Whatever its name, it is achingly beautiful. Formed by the artistry, imagination, and creativity of God, how could it be otherwise? Its colors are startlingly vivid. Life seems to spring up in abundance everywhere. Even in its natural wildness it seems to exhibit an orderliness, a feeling of structure and purpose, but expressed in profuse and infinitely changing variety. You feel you could explore the intricate wonder of this place for a thousand years and still daily come across new marvels.

As you walk through this landscape you become aware of others around you. You realize that however beautiful your surroundings may have seemed at first, they pale in comparison to these creatures of glory. These people are breathtaking. The place through which you are walking may well be a work of God's art, but the people walking with you are somehow bearers of God's very life and breath. To look on one of them is to gaze into the face of God, and it is magnificent. Every one of them has a beauty that could bring you to tears, were you to look on it clearly enough and long enough.

And then you stop, startled, as you realize that there are others who look at you and see exactly the same: someone beautiful, someone glorious, someone magnificent in whom God dwells and delights. You take a few minutes to let that sink in.

Imagine you slowly become aware that these others are not simply wandering around, they are engaging in all manner of activities. You notice artists of every kind: musicians in their orchestras, players in quartets and bands, and singers in choirs. There are sculptors, painters, glassblowers, weavers, embroiderers, and photographers. Dancers leap around one another and around you. Poets recite to one another, and writers trace limpid prose onto their pages. You see architects studying their blueprints with construction workers.

Construction workers? Yes, there is artistry of every kind going on here; creativity, endeavor, the shaping of the world in every way. Lumberjacks cut trees and prepare the wood for building. Masons shape stone. A blacksmith at the forge heats and bends metal into strange and wonderful forms. In the shell of a rising building you notice plumbers, electricians, decorators at work.

The varieties of work seem endless. You see chefs and cooks preparing meals, teachers instructing children, farmers plowing the fields, and baristas preparing steaming coffee. And alongside the workers you notice others occupied very differently: runners, swimmers, cyclists, youngsters playing ball games, someone reading, another simply lying in a field watching the clouds overhead. People just enjoying being alive in this beautiful place.

As you watch all this activity, you gradually begin to realize that among all this runs a single golden thread: *love*. This is how these people are able to show love for one another. By creating beautiful art. By building homes and schools. By teaching, by cooking, by growing food, by delighting in one another's company and in the world around them. You begin to see, behind the endless variety of seemingly random activity, the unifying presence of the community of love.

Perhaps a tiny nagging doubt pesters at the back of your mind: Why aren't these people gathered together in some gigantic temple, surrounding God and endlessly singing hymns and chanting psalms? Isn't that what heaven is supposed to be all about? Why isn't eternity more religious, less obviously secular?

While you're wondering where you might find God in the midst of all this, you start noticing something else: God seems to be right here already, manifest all around you. Like the gentle breeze blowing through the trees, the Spirit of God is everywhere present and moving through all these lives and these activities.

As you continue to explore, you become conscious also of this: that these people are *constantly* expressing their love toward God. Some of them are gathered together and singing hymns. But others are loving God by loving those around them, those in whom they know God's life so wonderfully dwells. Some are loving God by delighting in his creativity, and some by echoing that creativity in their own. But these people together are singing a great song of love, in words and music and silence and action and stillness, a song that rings through all creation and says: in life, in love, in one another, and in you, God—we rejoice!

But there is another song that runs around this hymn of the people, a song that weaves its harmonies through the skies and seems to tremble under the earth itself, the hymn of joy and delight that brought this place into being from the beginning and continues to sustain it. You still yourself to listen more closely. This song is *astonishing* in its utter beauty. It is ravishing. You feel as though your heart will burst open with every unfolding note. It unlocks a deep longing in the very center of your being, a longing to hear this song more deeply, more fully, to let it soak into your flesh and bones.

From the moment you begin to hear it, you start framing your life around that deeper song, the song of ravishment and delight. Wherever it can most clearly be heard, you go. You notice that it seems clearer and purer when you are with certain people, so you spend more time with them. As you love them more deeply you find the song rises in its joyful intensity even more, so you open your heart as much as you can and love them without reserve. Sometimes the song seems to respond to your singing, so you sing yourself hoarse; at other times it is fullest in your silence, so you learn to keep perfect stillness.

You know this song. It is the song of God. In this place, people have discovered how to make their lives an offering of joy and delight to God. But God also sings over them. You are learning to experience *his* joy and delight in all that he has made. In the beauty of all that is, in people, and in you. Yes, in you. You are discovering the delight of God in you, and in his song you have also discovered yourself: your value, your worth, your purpose, your significance, your identity. Finally, enraptured in love with God and entirely given in love to others, you have found *you*. And you have become free and happy and complete.

Imagine this place.

Now imagine one more thing. Imagine that this is *not* the day after your death. Instead, it is today. This is not your dream of heaven; it is God's dream of creation, a dream made real by his limitless power. You already live in this achingly beautiful dream; you dwell in eternity now. At this moment you are surrounded by people made in his glorious image, and they are magnificent. They are capable of the greatest love, and they can express that in a thousand different ways in the ordinary business of daily life: in their art, their work, their neighborhoods, and their family life. They are worthy of your love. And all through the dream of creation God is singing his song of ravishing delight for those with ears to hear. There are ways you can open your soul to that song: places where it is more easily heard, practices that attune the ear of your heart, people who will help you listen. And in that song you can discover who you really are, even *become* who you really are.

Do you know where to find the dream of eternity? Take a good look out of the window. Hear the gospel whisper in your ear: "the kingdom of God has come to you" (Luke 11:20).

Let's explore.

1

THE
INVITATION

*We accept Jesus' invitation
to participate in God's
community of love.*

God-Soaked Creation

Broken People

God's Delight

Over to You

GOD-SOAKED CREATION

LONG EONS AGO, WHEN TIME AND SPACE were newly born and the cosmos burst into being, on the day the stars began to sing and the galaxies started to turn, when creation sprang into being, and for all the vast span of eternity before that day, God had a purpose for this universe. He had an unwavering, fixed intention that encompassed all existence and every person who has ever lived, and that purpose remains unchanged to this day. God is creating a community of love. That is his fixation and passion. He is shaping and molding a community of loving people in which he himself can dwell, described in the Bible as God's *family* or *household*, his *nation* and *people*. It is the community Jesus called the "kingdom of God." And you are invited to be part of it.

FROM THE BEGINNING

God's entire thought and will is bent toward bringing this community into being. His intention is written into every page of Scripture, from the first to the last, from the opening pages of the book of Genesis to the closing chapters of John's great vision in Revelation.

Let's start at the beginning. Genesis 1 opens with a poetic tour de force describing the transforming and redemptive power of God at work. The story opens with the earth already in place but "a formless void" (v. 2): *formless*, and therefore chaotic and purposeless; *void*, and therefore empty and lifeless. The surface of the planet was covered by the shifting, restless waters. To the Hebrews, who were never much for sea travel, this endless ocean evoked a sense of danger and death. But a new story was about to be written, for the Spirit of God "swept over the face of the waters" (v. 2).

God spoke and creation responded. Light was separated from darkness; the waters below (the seas) and those above (the rain-filled clouds) were split apart to create the skies; and dry land was called forth in the midst of the oceans. The earth was given shape and structure, became a place where meaningful and purposeful life could be experienced. And yet it remained empty, barren, lifeless.

So God spoke again, and again creation responded. In the realm of separated light and darkness he called forth the sun, moon, and stars, believed by the ancients to be living and divine creatures: in other words, God filled darkness and light with life. Then he summoned life into the separated skies and seas, bringing into being the fish and birds. Finally the dry land was populated with all manner of creatures, from beetles and bacteria to lions and elephants.

God did—well, God did what God always does: took a chaotic mess, something dead and cold, and breathed his Spirit over it to bring order, sense, meaning, and an overwhelming and exuberant out-pouring of life itself.

But for God the shaping of this magnificent cosmos was not an end in itself; it had a further and very definite purpose. It was, of course, already astonishingly beautiful; to this day the unnecessary beauty of the natural world around us continues to bear witness to God's profound creativity, imagination, and joy in all that he has made. But creation was not merely an ecstatic flourish of artistic energy. God had an intention for his new world: he was making room for a unique expression of his own self and nature. This world was to be both a place drenched in God's holy presence and a dwelling for human beings living in relationship with him and with one another. Creation, a space opened up in which we could live and flourish, was God's great act of hospitality.

And so, as his culminating creative act,

> God created humankind in his image,
>> in the image of God he created them;
>> male and female he created them. (Genesis 1:27)

In both tellings of our origins found in Genesis (the first in Genesis 1:1–2:3, the second in Genesis 2:4-25), human beings are created from the beginning in community: as men and women sharing life together. We can see in this a reflection of God's own eternal nature. As little as we understand what it means for God to exist as Trinity—as Father, Son, and Spirit, distinct from one another yet sharing the same nature and indwelling each other as one God—as poorly as we comprehend this, we see that relationship is the essence of God's nature, just as it is central to our own being and identity. God, who exists in community, created from the beginning not isolated individuals but community.

TO THE LAST DAY—AND BEYOND

God's deliberate intention continues right through the pages of Scripture to the very last chapter. He called families: Abraham and Sarah, Isaac and Rebekah, Jacob and Rachel. He called a nation: the Israelites. He called all peoples into the kingdom announced by Jesus.

And the Bible closes with a magnificent vision of a new Jerusalem standing at the very heart of a renewed creation, a healed and restored heaven and earth. The final pages of Scripture ask us to imagine a city of almost unimaginable proportions. If we step away from the language of vision and dream for a moment and picture this city as concrete and real, here is what we see: lay the eastern edge of the city on the eastern seaboard of the United States and its western wall would rest near the Rocky Mountains, its northern border would be in Canada, and its southern gates open into the Gulf of Mexico. And since the city is built as a giant cube, most of its layers would reach far beyond the atmosphere and lie out in the vacuum of space. It's a fantastically generous vision of new community on a breathtaking scale, a city large enough to accommodate in comfort every man, woman, and child who has ever lived and with plenty of room to spare. And this, we are told, is where God himself chooses to dwell, right in the midst of this great city. "I saw no temple in the city," writes the apostle John, "for its temple is the Lord God" (Revelation 21:22).

Everything God has done from the moment of creation, and everything God will do until the end of time, is focused on the formation of a magnificent, all-encompassing God-soaked loving community. *Everything*. It is his sole focus, his passion, his obsession.

HERALDED BY JESUS

It's no surprise, then, to discover that when Jesus begins preaching openly in Galilee, his message begins with the announcement of God-soaked community: "The time is fulfilled, and the kingdom of God has come near" (Mark 1:15). In all Jesus' teaching and preaching God's community of love, the *kingdom of God* was a constantly recurring theme.

Jesus spent his time traveling from town to town in order to preach the kingdom (Luke 4:43), and he later sent out his followers on the same mission: "to proclaim the kingdom of God and to heal" (Luke 9:2). He taught his disciples that he had given them the secrets of the kingdom (Luke 8:10) and that they should pray for its realization among them: "[may] your kingdom come" (Matthew 6:10).

He told stories about the nature of the kingdom, comparing it to a tiny seed that grew unexpectedly into a great plant (Matthew 13:31-32), a treasure hoard discovered buried in a field (Matthew 13:44), a fishing net that sweeps up people from around the world (Matthew 13:47-50), and so much more. (These three examples are from just one chapter of a single Gospel!)

He argued that his miracles revealed that already "the kingdom of God has come to you" (Luke 11:20) and that people should seek this kingdom above all else in this world (Matthew 6:33). When he was put on trial and executed by the Roman and Jewish authorities, it wasn't for the religious crime of heresy, but the social and political crime of sedition: he was crucified for announcing a new kingdom, a rival social order to that of Rome (John 18:33-37). The kingdom, God's loving community, was so much the heart of Jesus' teaching, preaching, and mission that ultimately it became the cause for which he was willing to be betrayed and killed.

LIVING KINGDOMS

It's easy for us, living in a very different world from that of first-century Palestine, to misunderstand all this talk about the "kingdom." There's something archaic about the language; we might picture territorial lines drawn on some parchment map being pored over by armored knights while their steely-eyed monarch watches from his magnificent throne. Kingdoms seem to have more to do with Arthurian jousting or Tolkien's elves than with our contemporary world of polling booths and global commerce.

Like just under a tenth of the world's population, though, I grew up (and still live) in a modern kingdom—in my case, the United Kingdom of Great Britain and Northern Ireland. I remember the street party we held, when I was a young boy, to celebrate Queen Elizabeth's Silver Jubilee; we hung bunting from the lampposts and laid out trestle tables groaning with food along the length of the road under a bright summer sun. As a boy scout I renewed my oath every week to "do my best, to do my duty to God and the Queen, and to help other people." My father and stepfather served in Her Majesty's Royal Navy doing their bit "for Queen and country." To this day we Brits send letters in the Royal Mail, licking and sticking stamps adorned with the monarch's head onto the corner of the envelope; we pay taxes to Her Majesty's government; we buy pastries and coffee in the local cafe using coins and notes issued by the Royal Mint imprinted with the Queen's image. Reminders that we live in this kingdom surround us everywhere we look.

But for most of us, most of the time, all this is only tangentially about power and authority, or territory and maps. The kingdom I belong to is, above all, a community of people: my family and loved ones, my friends and neighbors, my colleagues and acquaintances, and the millions of fellow citizens whose lives are more distantly connected with mine. The monarch is perhaps best understood less as a ruler and more as a symbol of this huge society and all it represents. Her Majesty's government regulates the community, her armed forces protect it, the Royal Mail helps to keep it connected. But it's the people who *make* it. Sure, we have what Winston Churchill called "this sceptred isle" on which we spend most of our time, but even the land isn't the kingdom: when I travel abroad, I'm still a subject and citizen, still connected to my people and community. The United Kingdom is who we are together, not where we live.

This is the kind of kingdom Jesus proclaimed; this is what God had in mind from the very first moment of creation: *community*. A God-soaked community of people whose lives are defined not by territories and authorities, by shifting allegiances to political systems and philosophies, but by deep bonds of love to one another and to their Creator. Rulers and nations come and go. The poet Shelley, in his great poem "Ozymandias," describes a vast monument to a forgotten dictator in the Middle East carrying a hubristic inscription:

"My name is Ozymandias, king of kings:
Look on my works, ye Mighty, and despair!"
Nothing beside remains. Round the decay
Of that colossal wreck, boundless and bare
The lone and level sands stretch far away.

The mightiest cities will one day crumble, and the most noble societies will pass. But God's purpose remains steadfast and cannot be frustrated. God, whose presence fills all creation, is calling people to life in a community built on eternal foundations. He is calling you.

BROKEN PEOPLE

OVER THE CENTURIES that followed Jesus' first proclamation of this God-soaked community, people began to speak and think about the kingdom in other terms. For some it became a convenient shorthand for a new religion, *Christianity* (a word which never appears in the Gospels), or for the *church* (which is mentioned only twice, in Matthew's Gospel). Others picked up on the political color behind "kingdom" language, with its overtones of authority, power, and control. Eventually the "kingdom of God" became confused with the medieval ideal of Christendom, a social imposition of religious dogmas and institutions on a national scale—Christianity, church, and political society all rolled into one.

But Jesus never proclaimed the kingdom as a new religion. Jesus was a Jew born into an impeccable Jewish line, a descendant of David the king and a member of the ancient and noble tribe of Judah. Like most Jewish boys of his time (and every generation since) he was instilled with the traditions, beliefs, worship, and practices of Judaism: he was circumcised, he studied and observed Scripture, he worshiped in the synagogue and temple, and he kept Passover and other annual festivals. He bluntly told his disciples: "Do not think that I have come to abolish the law or the prophets; I have not come to abolish but to fulfill. . . . Unless your righteousness exceeds that of the scribes and Pharisees, you will never enter the kingdom of heaven" (Matthew 5:17, 20).

Even Paul, the most energetic supporter of the growth of the Jesus movement beyond the Jewish community into the wider Gentile world, never suggested that he was presenting a new religion to replace Judaism; instead he believed that Jesus had expanded the frontiers of the original Jewish community to create space alongside Jews for Gentiles too, so that both together could share in the promises of God. Writing to the Gentile believers in Rome, he compared them to wild olive branches grafted into the "rich root" of a cultivated tree, and urged them to "remember that it is not you who support the root, but the root that supports you" (Romans 11:17-18). For Jesus, the kingdom of God was not a new religion.

Nor was the kingdom a new religious institution: a church to replace the synagogue, the temple, or the people of Israel. Certainly Jesus criticized abuses in all these expressions of organized faith: abuses of power, of moral authority, of wealth and influence. He spoke against the hypocrisy that seems too often to be endemic among religious leadership. But he speaks only twice of the *ekklēsia*, the congregation (a word which elsewhere in the New Testament is most frequently used to describe the church), and on both those occasions (Matthew 16:18; 18:17) the Gospel writer is simply translating into Greek the Aramaic word for an assembly or gathering; it is almost certainly used by Jesus to describe the early community of his followers. The church may well participate in the kingdom or express the kingdom, but it can no more be *identified* with the kingdom than Christianity can.

Above all else, the kingdom was not a new political entity. Whatever the merits and failures of medieval Christendom, it was not simply the embodiment of the kingdom of God in European social and political life. Jesus strongly discouraged his disciples from taking up positions of leadership and authority (Matthew 20:25-28); when the crowds were tempted to promote him as their preferred king he hid himself from them (John 6:15); and at his trial he bluntly informed Pilate: "My kingdom is not from this world" (John 18:36). The kingdom of God was not, for Jesus, first and foremost a political reality (although it had deep political *implications*, which we'll explore later).

The kingdom Jesus proclaimed was neither Christianity, church, nor Christendom (words that carry all kinds of unhelpful associations in the minds of many people, and that we'll seek to avoid using here in our exploration of Jesus' teaching about a God-soaked life). Above all else, Jesus understood the kingdom to be a *community*—that amazing divine and human community of loving friendship that God had envisioned from the beginning of all creation, and that has remained his constant and central purpose through all the unfolding ages since.

GOD OF LOVE AND COMMUNITY

Really, it could hardly have been otherwise. After all, loving community is rooted in the very being of God; it's his essential nature.

The Hebrew Scriptures had always insisted clearly, in a world filled with polytheistic religions, on the unique individuality of God. The *Shema*, the great Jewish creedal prayer recited daily by all the devout, begins with the words: *Sh'ma Yisra'eil, Adonai Eloheinu, Adonai echad*, quoting the book of Deuteronomy: "Hear, O Israel: The LORD is our God, the LORD alone" (Deuteronomy 6:4). Judaism is a fiercely monotheistic faith: God is not simply a great God, one among many divine beings, not even the strongest and superior god. There is simply one God and none other.

So it was shocking to Jesus' contemporaries when he spoke about himself as God's Son (see, for example, John 3:35), which they understood as a claim to divinity (John 5:18). He called God "Abba" (Mark 14:36), an intimate Aramaic word for "Father," which almost certainly lies behind the opening line of the Lord's Prayer, "Our Father" (Matthew 6:9). He also spoke about the Holy Spirit as distinct from both himself and the Father: "the Advocate, the Holy Spirit, whom the Father will send in my name, will teach you everything" (John 14:26).

This left the first followers of Jesus with a real problem; they held firmly to the belief that *Adonai echad*: the Lord is one. But they had come to experience that one Lord in Jesus, and in God whom Jesus had taught them to call "Father," and in the Spirit present in their day-to-day lives. The complex picture is perhaps best illustrated in the story of Jesus' baptism: as Jesus came out of the river Jordan, the Spirit alighted on him in the form of a dove, and the voice of the Father spoke from heaven. There is only one Lord, the first followers claimed, but we see the Lord in all these three.

Over the centuries people wrestled with this paradox, and the idea that emerged was that God was best understood as Trinity: three persons sharing a single essence or nature. Simply put, the followers of Jesus opted to preserve the paradox and continue to speak of God as both three and one; they then developed ever more nuanced ways of explaining and exploring that extraordinary idea. And one of its key implications was this: that God is *essentially* relational. In other words, relationships are not something God *does*, relationship is what God *is*; it is one of the fundamental characteristics of God's nature. As John expresses it in his first letter: "God is love" (1 John 4:16). Notice that he doesn't write "God loves" but "God *is* love." We'll explore some of the implications of this later in this book.

There is great depth to this mystery, more than we can truly understand (if we're honest). But if we can grasp the central idea, that the nature of God in Trinity is essentially relationship, then we can begin to understand why the defining character of God's kingdom is relationship: God's relationship with human beings and our relationships with one another. Creation simply reflects the nature of its maker.

A COMMUNITY OF THE LEAST AND LOST

At the center of every kingdom we find the king, usually a figure of great majesty exalted above the wider community by his magnificence and splendor. At the heart of God's kingdom we also come face to face with one to whom "every knee should bend, in heaven and on earth and under the earth" (Philippians 2:10). But when he described his vision of the heavenly court, the contemplative apostle John spoke of seeing "between the throne and the four living creatures and among the elders a Lamb standing as if it had been slaughtered" (Revelation 5:6). He was glimpsing the astonishing truth that God's kingdom is a community of the broken ruled over by a wounded king.

In his teaching and in his life Jesus utterly subverted the presumptions of authority and hierarchy prevalent in every other human kingdom. The kingdom of God announced by Christ was a community that mirrored and echoed God's love, and the striking characteristics of divine love—grace, mercy, forgiveness, mutual service, sacrifice, and more—are also the defining characteristics of the relationships that form the substance of this kingdom. And more than this, Jesus took the foundation stones of every kingdom the world had yet seen and broke them open to reveal something entirely new and unexpected: a kingdom overshadowed by the cross.

In Jesus' teaching it is always the last, the least, and the lost who stand at the very center of kingdom life. The kingdom belongs to both the "poor in spirit" and those "persecuted for righteousness' sake" (Matthew 5:3, 10). The movers and shakers of this world were warned bluntly: "How hard it is for those who have wealth to enter the kingdom of God! Indeed, it is easier for a camel to go through the eye of a needle than for someone who is rich to enter the kingdom of God" (Luke 18:24-25). But while the powerful struggle to enter, a multitude of the least in this world flood in. "People will come from east and west, from north and south," said Jesus, "and will eat in the kingdom of God. Indeed, some who are last will be first, and some are first who will be last" (Luke 13:29-30).

During one of the persecutions that afflicted the early church, the prefect of Rome arrested a young deacon called Lawrence. The prefect knew that one of Lawrence's responsibilities was the care of

his congregation's property, and he demanded that Lawrence arrange
to hand over all the wealth of church. Lawrence asked for three days
to comply, time that he used to prepare for his next meeting with the
authorities. After the three days had passed Lawrence came into the
prefect's presence surrounded by beggars and paupers: the lame and
blind, the maimed and outcast, the widows and orphans gathered up
from the backstreets of Rome. Lawrence waved his hand grandly over
the pathetic crowd. "Here they are!" he announced. "Our pride, our
glory, our treasure. I offer them to you. Behold, prefect: here is the
wealth of the church!"

A KINGDOM POOR AND SMALL

This community of the broken arrives in humility, in simplicity and
smallness. The kingdom is not imposed as an act of power from on
high; it is offered as a gift of love. How could it be otherwise? To
demand love is to destroy love. So the coming of the kingdom is
gentle and easily missed, not at all the sounding trumpets and fiery
chariots from heaven we might expect. Jesus proclaimed the arrival
of the kingdom, but it came not to subdue us—rather to invite us to
the quiet surrender of our hearts. It is like the smallest of all seeds
(Matthew 13:31-32), like yeast sprinkled on dough (Matthew 13:33),
like hidden treasure (Matthew 13:44), like a child (Matthew 18:3-4).
In this kingdom the greatest are those who serve (Luke 22:26); your
life is only found as you lay it aside (Matthew 10:39); seeds grow only
as they fall and die (John 12:24); the footsteps of the King lead to
crucifixion (Mark 8:34).

The kingdom of God can be found wherever men and women find
their center in their loving relationships with God and with one another. This makes it unlike any other society or community on earth.
Jesus lived in a culture where political kingdoms were very real. But
he consistently preached an alternative vision of reality: another
kingdom that was gently but insistently making itself visible in the

world and courting our allegiance. He invited people to define themselves through their relationship with God rather than with the Roman Emperor. "Give to the emperor the things that are the emperor's," he famously said, "and to God the things that are God's" (Mark 12:17). Caesar could make demands for the coins he manufactured with his image stamped on the surface. But God was making a wider and more sweeping claim: a claim on the person holding the coins, the person stamped with God's image. Caesar sought to exercise power and control, but God longs for our love.

It's no surprise, then, that when Jesus was asked which of the many commandments in Jewish law was the greatest, he immediately began to talk in terms of these relationships that lie at the heart of kingdom life. "Love the Lord your God with all your heart, and with all your soul, and with all your mind, and with all your strength," he replied, and "love your neighbor as yourself" (Mark 12:30-31). But he went further. Not only are these the two greatest commandments, he said, but in fact all the Law and the Prophets—every teaching in the Bible—hinges on these two commandments. The essence of life is our relationship with God and our relationships with one another; these are what define us. The invitation to life in the kingdom is an invitation to embrace those relationships in all their fullness.

GOD'S DELIGHT

OF COURSE, JESUS' INVITATION into the life of the kingdom was not only for the people living in the Holy Land in the first century; it is also for you and me. And it's not only for the saintly, the righteous, the holy among us. Jesus has thrown the gates of the kingdom wide and invites us all—the broken, the failures, the compromised, the bitter, the anguished, and the wicked, along with everyone else. Jesus offers us this invitation because of God's tremendous delight in us. God rejoices in our friendship, our companionship. He longs to shower love on us and to see us grow in our ability to love him and love one another. He made us for himself, and his heart is restless until it finds its rest in us.

I meet many people who find it difficult to believe that God might take such delight in them. When we look at ourselves in the mirror we can have very mixed feelings about the person looking back. Some seem to be fortunate enough to see the glory and magnificence God gave us at our creation. But many more are painfully aware of all the flaws and failings, the scars and disappointments, the distressing inadequacies. We may present ourselves to the world as winningly and positively as we can, but in private we can see what no one else sees. We all have a shadow side, and almost all of us are afraid of it.

It's easy to reason that if we see ourselves in this way, then God who sees everything and knows the hearts of all must see the same. I might accept the idea that God loves people, the human race in general, but it's harder to accept that God loves me. When I speak to some people about the delight of God, they are animated and excited by the idea, but find it astonishing, even shocking, to think of *themselves* as God's source of delight. I often quote a line written by the Indian Jesuit Anthony de Mello only to find people are scandalized by it: "Behold God beholding you . . . and smiling!"

Clearly, then, this idea of God's delight needs a little more exploration. I find it helpful to look at the stories of the baptism and transfiguration of Jesus. In many ways, these stories mirror the whole experience of kingdom life with God. The first illustrates the condition we find ourselves in when God invites us into relationship with him, the other the end God is always leading us toward. It's fascinating and instructive to compare them both.

HUMILIATION AND GLORY

The baptism of Jesus (Matthew 3:1-17) is a narrative in which most of us can easily discover ourselves. John the Baptist preached repentance to the great crowds who gathered on the banks of the Jordan. One after another he led people into the waters to be washed and made new, to cleanse themselves, to loosen their crabbed and tightly clenched hands and release the dirt and filth they'd been holding close for security, for pleasure, for comfort. And every penitent walking down off the banks stirred up the riverbed until the water itself was swirling with mud, a vivid image of all the wretchedness they hoped to wash away through this simple symbolic act.

When Jesus stepped down into this dirt and filth asking for baptism, John was appalled. "I need to be baptized by you!" he protested (Matthew 3:14), startled and confused that Christ would choose to immerse himself in these polluted waters. But Jesus insisted that this was necessary, that he must stand in solidarity with all these broken, lost, rebellious, vicious, withered, and hopeless souls. It's not hard for most of us to see Jesus standing in the Jordan and to understand that he is identifying with us, and that we are meant to identify ourselves with him. Here is the friend of sinners (Luke 7:34), the one made to be sin for us (2 Corinthians 5:21).

The transfiguration (Matthew 17:1-8) presents more of a challenge to our imagination. On that mountaintop, set apart from the everyday world, Jesus is radiant with the uncreated light of God and surrounded by the company of heaven (personified in the great pillars of the Old Testament, Moses and Elijah). This is a vision of Jesus that is seemingly unlike us in every respect, and is often taken as a revelation to the watching disciples of his previously veiled divine nature. This, we might say, is what God looks like.

But there is another ancient reading of this story. When "the Word became flesh and lived among us" (John 1:14), he had to conceal not only the full majesty of his divine nature but also the glory of his human nature. The people of Galilee and Jerusalem, like us, had never seen a human being untainted and unbroken. The wonder of God's image and likeness (Genesis 1:26) so fully revealed would have been overwhelming to them. So just as he veiled his divine nature, Christ also veiled something of his humanity—until this day on the mountain when he let the disciples see just how beautiful and magnificent a human being could be. This, he was showing them, is what a person is supposed to look like.

In the transfiguration, then, Jesus was not contrasting himself with us, setting the richness of his divinity against the poverty of our limited humanity. Rather he was offering the disciples an insight into the transformation the Spirit was working in them and would continue to work in people across the world over the centuries to come, a transformation that would only find its completion in eternity, but the beginnings of which would be apparent in our day-to-day existence here and now.

THE VOICE OF THE FATHER

These two stories, then, mark the limits of human possibility. Life in the kingdom is a journey from the first toward the second, an invitation

to begin at repentance for our brokenness (Mark 1:15) and be transformed by God's grace until we experience abundant life (John 10:10).
We recognize ourselves as we are now in the Christ of sinners, standing
in the Jordan; we are invited to recognize what we will be in the Christ
of beauty, standing in splendor on the mountain.

If that's the case, one aspect of these two narratives is particularly
striking. When Christ stands on the mountain revealed in his glory,
the voice of the Father speaks from heaven: "This is my Son, the
Beloved; with him I am well pleased" (Matthew 17:5). And is it any
wonder? He is breathtaking. We can easily imagine that if we were
able to shine with such radiance, the Father would also delight in us
and call us beloved.

But when we look back down the mountain to the Jordan, to the
filthy waters and the crowd of sinners, a surprise awaits us. Jesus came
up out of the river, the rank and polluted water pouring over him.
There was no light, no Moses and Elijah, no radiance and beauty. This
was Christ in weakness among the broken. But what do we hear
spoken by the Father from heaven? The very same words that were
spoken on the mountain: "This is my Son, the Beloved, with whom I
am well pleased" (Matthew 3:17).

We may hope to become identified with Christ in glory one day, to
become "participants of the divine nature" (2 Peter 1:4), to be completely reconciled, healed, and restored by the Spirit, and then to hear
ourselves called beloved sons and beloved daughters in whom the
Father is well pleased. But here is one of the wonders of the gospel: as
we stand alongside Christ of the sinners now, as we identify ourselves
completely with him among the lost, the wounded, the rebellious, and
the penitent—even now, before any transformation can possibly be
wrought in us, we hear this same voice: my son, my daughter, my
beloved, in whom I delight.

And from this delight emerges an invitation: Jesus is inviting us
to life in the community of God, a life that is abundant, deep, rich,

and flourishing. This is the life you were born to live, and the only life in which you will find real fulfilment and joy. It is a life of purpose and significance, of wonder and beauty. It is also a life of hardship, endeavor, suffering, and tears. Christ's invitation is not made lightly: it is born out of God's immense and costly love for you. And it is not an invitation to be accepted lightly: it will change you utterly, reaching into every corner of your life and encompassing your entire existence. Will you accept his invitation or not? This is the most fundamental decision you will ever make. And you face this question afresh every day you live.

OVER TO YOU

Scripture and Reflection

IN THESE OPENING PAGES we've considered the idea that God's purpose in all creation and history from the very beginning was the formation of a loving community that has God at its very heart, and that the loving relationships which make this community possible are simply a reflection of God's own essential nature. I've proposed that Jesus used the language of the "kingdom of God" to talk about this community, and that in his love for us God is inviting us to participate in the life of the kingdom. I've also suggested that this invitation stems from God's delight in us, a delight he continues to express despite all our obvious shortcomings and failings.

Before we continue, you may want to spend some time reflecting for yourself on some of the key passages in the Bible that relate to these ideas. You might also want to take time to mull over your own thoughts about the ideas we've explored so far. The following readings and questions are designed to help you think, pray, and consider. You might want to spend some time with one passage each day of the coming week, or you may simply want to look at one or two of these readings and questions that seem particularly helpful.

- *Ephesians 1:3-10*

  Why do you think there is *something* rather than *nothing*? What was God's purpose in creating the universe? Why does *anything* exist?

- *Genesis 1:1–2:4*

  Have you ever experienced God bringing meaning to chaos and filling what is lifeless with life? What did you learn about God through that experience?

- *Matthew 5:17-20*

  How clearly do you think the idea of the God-soaked community of love can be seen in the Hebrew Scriptures (the Old Testament)? Where is it hard to see?

- *Matthew 13:44-53*

  Why do you think the idea of the kingdom of God was so important to Jesus? How do you think *he* understood the kingdom?

- *Luke 17:20-21*

  What do you see in the world around you which suggests that the kingdom is already among us? What do you see that suggests it *isn't*? What do you make of these words of Jesus?

- *1 John 4:7-12*

  What does it mean to say that "God is love" (v. 8)? How does the idea of God as Trinity make that clearer or more confusing?

- *Proverbs 8:22-31*

  Why might God find himself "delighting in the human race" (v. 31)? Does God delight in you?

HEART RENEWAL

We seek the renewal of our hearts so we can love as Christ loves.

A New Heart

Love in Everything

Soul Healing

Over to You

A NEW HEART

I'M VERY GOOD AT GETTING THINGS WRONG. Decades of life experience have honed my capacity for screwing up into a fine art, as many people who know me have discovered to their cost. And with every passing year I see my flawed nature with increasing clarity. I'm not only great at messing up, I'm getting ever better at recognizing the roots of my problems within myself. You might think that would be a great gift: after all, it's only when we can really diagnose malfunctions that we can begin to address them, to fix them. The trouble is, as I'm constantly learning, it's one thing to see a problem. It's harder to accept it, to acknowledge it, and own it as your own. Harder still to *confess* it, to be open about your shortcomings with others, especially those most deeply affected by them. (How much easier it is to justify yourself and blame them instead!) But hardest of all is this: *change*.

One of the most glaringly difficult and painful issues Sally and I experienced in the early years of our marriage was my deep-seated aversion to conflict. It took a few months before that really raised its head, but as we began to work through the frictions of building a shared life from two very individual identities, conflicts inevitably flared up. And I instinctively responded using the psychological mechanism I'd developed from my youth, which I thought had served me so well: detaching myself until everything calmed down. Practitioners of family systems theory, following the work of Murray Bowen, talk about our natural inclination to respond to conflict either by fusing (collapsing our identity, emotions, and viewpoints into those of the people around us to make conflict impossible) or distancing (separating ourselves so far from other people that conflict becomes unsustainable). I chose to distance myself fantastically well at every opportunity: through silence and moodiness, through avoidance and changing the subject, or by simply physically walking away. I created a barrier that no conflict could penetrate.

It took some time before I realized the obvious: the barriers I created also made *resolution* and *relationship* impossible too. Whenever I distanced myself from Sally, I could nurse my grievances in peace— but never have them challenged and transformed. It took a long time to realize this, and longer still to begin to address it. Looking back now I understand that, for her, this was part of the challenge of fulfilling her marriage vows: to remain committed to loving me until I was ready to stay put and work things out.

It was hard to recognize that, and harder still to be open about it with Sally. Hard, especially, to admit that maybe—maybe!—I hadn't always been in the right in every single disagreement we'd had over the course of our life together, and so humbling to acknowledge that my *response* to those disagreements was itself a key part of the difficulty we had in resolving them. But what has proved hardest of all has been *change*. I still feel the challenge of that to this day. Every time we argue, I feel the cost, the pain, the struggle of simply staying put, not walking away, enduring the discomfort of our conflict while we work it through. I've been known to storm out of the room, only to stomp back a few minutes later to say, gruffly, "No. I want to walk away, but I can't. I don't want to be here right now, and I don't want to talk about this, but I know I need to, and you know it too."

I'm still very much a work in progress, even after a quarter of a century of marriage. It seems I've not yet finished learning my lessons. Even now, I don't always come back.

A HARD INVITATION

In the Gospels Jesus presented the good news about God's kingdom together with a profound challenge. People responded with enthusiasm and joy to Jesus' invitation to life in God's astonishing community of love. "Immediately they left their nets and followed him," we are told of Simon and Andrew (Mark 1:18). "He saw a man called Matthew sitting at the tax booth," reads another report, "and he said to him, 'Follow me.' And he got up and followed him" (Matthew 9:9). Zacchaeus initially hid from Jesus in the leaves of a sycamore tree, but when Christ called him "he hurried down and was happy to welcome him" (Luke 19:6), an act of hospitality that transformed his life. Crowds followed Jesus wherever he went; on one occasion he had his disciples get a boat ready "because of the crowd, so that they would not crush him" (Mark 3:9); within days he was back home in Capernaum and "the crowd came together again, so that they could not even eat" (Mark 3:20). The blind, lame, diseased, and crippled pressed in on him seeking healing; those plagued by evil or by the bitterness of their own conscience sought him out; he was constantly surrounded by sinners, outcasts, the dregs of society to whom he proclaimed the hope of a fresh start, new life in God's new community. Almost all Jesus' contemporaries instinctively understood that this kingdom was *good news*, and they welcomed it with alacrity.

But the challenge quickly followed: life in this new community required deep, far-reaching change of heart and mind, death to a former way of life in order to discover a new road, a profound reorientation of a person's whole existence. This challenge lay at the heart of Jesus' message from the very beginning. The Gospel writers summed up his preaching in two terse lines that we have already encountered: "The time is fulfilled, and the kingdom of God has come near; repent, and believe in the good news" (Mark 1:15).

RENEWAL OF THE HEART

The word translated "repent" (*metanoia*) here has less to do with confessing our wrongdoings and much more to do with an internal change of mind and heart. A simplistic, literal rendering of the word would be "to change one's mind," but it really has much deeper and richer overtones than this brief definition might suggest.

Jesus was not asking people simply to reconsider a few of their religious beliefs, to change a couple of lines in their personal creed or adopt a slightly adjusted philosophy. We might capture the sense more closely by paraphrasing this word as "change your entire outlook on life, the worldview that shapes everything you think and do." A person who becomes convinced of the value of whole wheat rather than white bread, or who finds in middle age that they have come to enjoy reading Shakespeare despite unpleasant memories of studying his works at school, has changed their mind, but they have not experienced *metanoia*. Instead we should picture someone who has left their lucrative job in high finance to become a communist agitator, or who has abandoned their leadership of a far-right white supremacy movement to work as a liberal and progressive equal rights lawyer. These are changes of mind that would affect every aspect of that person's life: their relationships, their lifestyle, their allegiances, their worldview, their very sense of identity. To repent is to experience a change of outlook and perspective that reshapes you from the heart outward and leaves no part of your life untouched.

The immensity of this realignment of life was recognized quickly by those who responded to Jesus with such initial enthusiasm. At first, the crowds flocked to Jesus, drawn by his seemingly limitless power to bring healing to mind and soul. But they soon began to understand that the kingdom he announced stood in stark opposition to a way of life they were reluctant to surrender. One person sought to follow him without being ready to leave behind his former life; Jesus warned him bluntly, "No one who puts a hand to the plow and looks back is fit for the kingdom of God" (Luke 9:62). A rich young man, confronted with the hold his wealth had over his heart, found himself unable to relinquish his riches and "went away grieving, for he had many possessions" (Matthew 19:22). As the crowds began to sense the profound reorientation required for life in the kingdom, they complained: "This teaching is difficult; who can accept it?" and many turned back; when Jesus asked his closest disciples whether they would stay or go, Simon Peter replied, "Lord, to whom can we go? You have the words of eternal life" (John 6:60-68)—a commitment of sorts, but hardly a resounding certainty of purpose.

The problem might become clear to us if we simply ask, am I a person who could live well in the kingdom of God proclaimed by Jesus? If the kingdom is a community of people living in relationships of great love for one another, a community with God himself at its very heart as source and sustainer of that love, then clearly only a profoundly loving person will be able to flourish and live abundantly in that community. Those who are unloving, self-centered, turned away from God and from others would wreak havoc and damage wherever they trod and would chafe against the character of the kingdom at every turn. The experience of trying to live an unloving life in a deeply loving community would be painful and purgatorial. We may as well try to push our way into the kingdom unchanged— which many do, in one way or another; as Jesus observed, "the kingdom of heaven has suffered violence, and the violent take it by force" (Matthew 11:12). But the violent can never be at ease once they are there; the very nature of the kingdom opposes everything they are.

Only those who are wholly loving can live well and joyfully within the kingdom. The unloving would find themselves miserable and afflicted even as they stood within the very walls of paradise. But here is our problem, and here is where the challenge of Jesus' proclamation bites us most painfully: we are precisely those deeply self-centered and unloving people. More so, perhaps, than many of us are prepared to admit, certainly more so than we usually realize.

LOVE IN
EVERYTHING

I SHOULD SAY RIGHT AWAY THAT, in one sense, it's impossible for us to be unloving people; the concept is as meaningless an oxymoron as an incorporeal body or valueless wealth. A human being is a creature of love, and we are helpless to do anything other than love.

This sounds like an outrageous suggestion in a world that has seen Auschwitz, the Rwandan genocide, global terrorism, world wars, the brutality of apartheid, and so much more suffering and horror inflicted by people against one another. We carry scars in our cultural memory: the vivid images of an expanding mushroom cloud, of nine-year-old Kim Phuc running terrified from a napalm attack in Vietnam, of the twin towers crumbling into dust and fire. How can we even speak of love in the face of such appalling suffering and viciousness?

I'm not always sure that we can. It's difficult, sometimes, for us to say anything at all in response to these horrors; there are certainly times when we simply need to shut up and weep with those who weep. But eventually we have to reconsider what it means to follow Jesus, to live a God-soaked life in the community of the kingdom, in a world in which such things are possible. How can we continue to speak of love, of a loving God, and of loving people?

And yet followers of Jesus have dared to do so, fully aware of the challenge. And perhaps that's because, over time, we've come to understand love not as an emotionally warm feeling toward another person, but rather as a deep cosmic power that shapes our lives and all creation with a forcefulness difficult to imagine. We've come to believe that love has the power to reshape the universe as we know it, for good but also for ill. Because the crucial question is not *whether* we love or not; in the end we cannot escape our own nature. We will love. We're helpless to do otherwise. No, the crucial question is this: *what* will we love—and what will our loving do to us and to the world around us?

GOD IS LOVE

We saw in an earlier chapter that the essence of God, his fundamental nature, is love. So our creation in the image and likeness of God imparts that essence, that character and nature, to us. Love is the raw matter of our spirit, our inner person, as surely as atoms are the raw matter of the body. The second creation narrative in Genesis describes this powerfully and poetically. God, we are told, plants a garden in the East and, within its gates, shapes the dust and dirt of the earth into a human body, a physical form. Then God "breathed into his nostrils the breath of life; and the man became a living being" (Genesis 2:7). In Hebrew thought a person's breath, the surest sign of life in the body, was identified with their spirit, their inner nature; the same word, *ruach*, was used for both. The animating life force breathed into Adam, his spirit, was the breath and Spirit of God, God's essential nature and character. Adam was animated by love. So from the beginning, God-created and God-enlivened people would love by instinct; if they simply did what came naturally to them in any circumstance, it would be the most loving action possible, because love was their nature.

And in a certain sense that is still the case. What can lovers do other than love? To be sure, we are corrupted lovers. Our spirits are warped, twisted, broken, depraved, sometimes collapsed or shattered. Our love has been turned in every wrong direction, diminished or magnified out of proportion, misapplied and misused. In some people and some societies the expressions of love that result lead to horror, to terrors and abominations that cause in others fear, bewilderment, and disgust in equal measure. But however defaced or ugly love may become, it remains love in some form. Evil is always a bending, forcing, breaking, or corruption of what God has made, of what is good and holy and beautiful; there is no source of creation in this cosmos other than God, no power capable of bringing forth *evil* as something new and unknown to God. There is no spiritual alchemy able to transmute love into something fundamentally different. You can melt gold or beat it into new shapes; you can bury it, stain it, spit on it; you can shape it into images of obscenity or magnificent works of art. But none of this changes its essential nature: it remains gold. In just the same way, our inner essence is love, regardless of what we do, what we have done to us, or who we become as a result.

TWISTED LOVE

So when we speak of people—or of ourselves—becoming loveless or unloving, we are really describing this corruption and depravity of love within us. And in the centuries after Jesus first issued his invitation to participate in the kingdom of God the first generations of his followers began to articulate with ever increasing precision the soul sickness within us that prevents us from participating in that kingdom. As physicians of the spirit, they learned to diagnose the maladies that made it impossible for us to be the kind of loving people who might flourish in the kingdom, who might "have life, and have it abundantly" (John 10:10).

Their starting point was a description of the human condition offered by John in his first letter:

> If you see your brother or sister committing what is not a mortal sin, you will ask, and God will give life to such a one—to those whose sin is not mortal. There is sin that is mortal; I do not say that you should pray about that. All wrongdoing is sin, but there is sin that is not mortal. (1 John 5:16-17)

The Greek phrase used by John in his letter literally means "deathward sin" or "sin that leads to death." In the medieval Latin translation of the Bible that became "peccatum ad mortem,"which led to the English rendering "mortal sins" or even "deadly sins."The implication of this short passage seemed to be that, while all soul-sickness matters, certain maladies of the spirit are so deep and pervasive that they are analogous to terminal illnesses in the body. Left unchecked and unhealed, they will ravage the soul and bring about its destruction: they affect our being at its root and thread their poison throughout the whole person. They also became known as the "cardinal sins"from the Latin word *cardo*, meaning a hinge: these diseases infected the pivots around which a person's whole life could be turned for good or for ill.

THE ANATOMY OF SIN

Over time various attempts to delimit these heart disorders were consolidated and integrated until a more or less definitive list of seven key ailments found a broad acceptance: a kind of "Grey's anatomy" of spiritual maladies. (The list still percolates through our contemporary culture as the "seven deadly sins.") It may be helpful to look at each of these mortal sicknesses in turn, to take a little time to identify each, in order to understand precisely how deeply and inescapably they seem to infect our societies, those around us, and our own hearts.

Pride is the most fundamental and far-reaching of all these conditions. It is the elevation of self to the heart of creation. Love turns inward, and we increasingly refer everything around us back to ourselves and to our own purposes and significance, as though the universe existed purely for our benefit and advancement. Pride, in societies, can lie at the root of excessive nationalism, xenophobia, and unbridled militarism; in individuals it often manifests as unbridled ambition, self-importance, or as simple discourtesy and arrogance.

Envy, another example of misdirected self-love, is content to assume a more humble and realistic station than pride would allow—but it still desires that its lower position be higher than anyone else's and can't abide the idea of being exceeded by others. Envy may not long to push us up the ladder, but it always desires to pull others down. In communities and societies this malady is often revealed as a resistance to excellence, a tendency to denigrate intellectual endeavor, to sneer at cultural and artistic achievement, to rejoice in toppling leaders and social icons, to despise wealth creators. In individuals, it is seen wherever we desire to tarnish the reputations of others, to undermine their achievements, or to block their advancement.

Wrath is the third of an unholy trinity of sicknesses grounded in misdirected self-love; it is the malice and violence we direct toward those we believe are frustrating the pursuit of our interests and advancements. Wrath seeks to damage, punish, or destroy all those who stand in the way of our own advancement. In society the realm of politics seems to be especially prone to expressions of both envy and wrath as the lure of power and influence leads many into an inhuman struggle for the top. For individuals, wrath can manifest itself in countless ways: road rage, anger about building projects near our homes, fury at successful peers promoted ahead of us. Anger against injustice can be a powerful emotion, but wherever that anger becomes directed toward individuals it is often a sign that wrath is not far away.

Sloth was known to the ancient writers as *accidie*, the Latin adaptation of a Greek word for a listless collapse of spiritual passion, an ennui of the soul. This is not love misdirected but love allowed to sleep, to fall dormant. In particular it referred to the slow cooling of our ardor for God and for the pursuit of life in his kingdom. Societies exhibit sloth or *accidie* when they cease to care about those things that most matter to community life, such as growth in knowledge and learning, the framing of just laws, devout spiritual life, or the pursuit of beauty in the arts. It can often be seen in individuals who seem directionless and lacking in energy or fire—for their work, their community life, and particularly for their life with God.

Avarice is neither a misdirection nor a lack of love. It is the first of three excesses of love: love directed precisely where it should be, but to an entirely inappropriate degree. Avarice is the inordinate love of the created world. God created the cosmos to be enjoyed and celebrated, to be a source of wonder and pleasure. But avarice seeks to reach out and grasp it, as though the material creation alone were capable of providing meaning, purpose, and worth. When societies are gripped with avarice they tend to reduce everything to measures of economic wealth, losing sight of the value of less tangible fields of human endeavor. Avaricious individuals come in many forms, including the hoarder, the miser, the materialist, and the playboy spendthrift.

Gluttony can be found wherever our consumption of the material world has become disordered, whether directly through food and drink, or less obviously through the consumption of goods and experiences. Again, this is an excess of an otherwise appropriate love. The joys of eating, drinking, using, playing, and experiencing have been allowed to become the substance and purpose of our lives. Communities and societies manifest gluttony whenever they tend toward hedonism and the unrestrained pursuit of pleasure. As individuals we can recognize gluttony in both excessive consumption—of food, drink, and material goods—and in excessive fastidiousness, the unwillingness to accept anything less than the finest wines and foods and the most luxurious goods.

Lust is a third excess of love; the physical and sexual pleasures we experience with other people, good in themselves, become magnified and distorted until they devour every other aspect of our relationships. We increasingly perceive others not as people but as objects of our pleasure, a perspective that tends rapidly toward the dehumanization of the other—a tendency seen clearly in the objectification inherent in pornography. Socially, lust tends to show itself in an ever-increasing and often gratuitous sexualization of daily life: in advertising, newspapers, television, movies, clothing, dance and music styles, the arts, even in everyday conversation. In individuals it can be seen wherever relationships are reduced to their physical and sexual dimensions alone, whether in a serial seducer cruising bars or in an isolated teenager surfing the less salubrious corners of the Internet.

We don't have to be monsters to recognize these disordered loves in our own hearts. Without being ravaged by boundless anger or unrestrained greed, most people have enough honesty and self-awareness to admit, even if only to themselves, that we are usually more ready to love ourselves than others, often allow our love for God and the world around us to lose its driving energy, and frequently find ourselves embracing the pleasures of this world in ways that are obsessive or unhealthy. We don't look into our hearts and find a well-balanced, outward-looking love in action. So if we were to find ourselves suddenly thrust into the midst of a society defined by its loving relationships with God, other people, and the world around us, we might discover ourselves to be deeply dysfunctional members of that society who caused damage, pain, and distress to ourselves and the wider community. We'd be a poor fit. In short, we're just not kingdom people. What can we do?

SOUL HEALING

THE GREAT SURPRISE ABOUT JESUS' INVITATION into the kingdom community was that it was addressed precisely to those who were most clearly not "kingdom people," to those in whom the maladies of disordered love were most evident. Other religious teachers challenged him when they saw that he surrounded himself with the scum of the earth and the dregs of society. "Those who are well have no need of a physician," he responded, "but those who are sick. . . . I have come to call not the righteous but sinners" (Matthew 9:12-13).

We seem to find that extravagant mercy so attractive and yet so difficult to grasp in reality. A friend of mine described being present in a service in an old Welsh chapel many decades ago when a young woman from the congregation was called forward to face a line of stern deacons gathered under the pulpit. She'd fallen pregnant outside of marriage, and the deacons had summoned her to face the discipline of the church. "You have brought shame on yourself," one of the deacons proclaimed gravely, "and shame on your family. You have brought shame on God. And what is worst of all, you have brought shame on this *chapel*."

She was expelled in humiliation. My friend also left that same day and never returned. He recalled sitting later that evening in the local pub over a pint, listening while the village drunk offered a philosophical reflection from his barstool: "Do you know why Jesus was born to an unmarried woman? So we'd know that God loves all the little bastards." And the sad reality was that this half-soaked drunk had understood the gospel more clearly than every one of the neatly polished deacons in that chapel.

When Jesus described himself as a *physician* to sinners, a *healer* of the inner life, he was calling himself much more than one who associated with the broken, more even than one who could and would forgive them for the damage they had wreaked in their relationships with God and one another. He was claiming to be one who could take damaged souls and restore them to health. He was offering to take their haywire and misguided loves, their hearts that strayed from one poorly chosen direction to another, and make them whole. To shape them into people whose inner life was so integrated and healthy that it quite naturally resulted in an outer life well lived, a life of virtue, integrity, meaning, purpose, and direction. He actively sought out the broken, not to pity them but to transform them.

This is an astonishing claim. The more shattered our souls are, the further we feel from any possibility of healing and wholeness. I once worked for a year in a church of the homeless. The members of that church were beautiful but deeply broken, struggling with severe personality disorders, mental illness, addictions, ingrained patterns of criminal behavior, a past history of neglect and abuse—in short, these were people who valued the idea of forgiveness but craved the hope of healing. And forgiveness at least seemed *possible*. Real, substantive change of heart and life felt unreachable. "I'm past saving," they would tell me, "just a lost cause."

It was to people like this that Jesus came, proclaiming the kingdom to every lost cause he ever met. He offered healing of the heart to the most savage sinner and every lost and terrified soul.

This transformation of the heart, this reorientation of love within us, is brought about in the same way we received God's loving nature within ourselves in the first place: through the breathing in of God's Spirit. In an echoing of the Genesis narrative of creation, Jesus stood among his disciples after his resurrection (the conquest of death itself, which is the ultimate negation of life and love), "breathed on them and said to them, 'Receive the Holy Spirit'" (John 20:22). This Spirit brings about our renewal and healing; Jesus tells his disciples that "it is the spirit that gives life" (John 6:63). Through the work of this Spirit within us, the image of God, reflected to us in the loving nature of Jesus, is reshaped and reconstituted in our souls, as Paul later wrote: "all of us ... seeing the glory of the Lord as though reflected in a mirror, are being transformed into the same image from one degree of glory to another; for this comes from the Lord, the Spirit" (2 Corinthians 3:18).

We are not healed by some titanic act of the will, a determined decision to leave behind our old ways and do better in the future—thank God, since this is beyond the reach of most of us anyway. Our problem is rooted in the very core of our being, as Jesus taught: "it is from within, from the human heart, that evil intentions come" (Mark 7:21); the disordering of love affects us so deeply within, we no longer have the spiritual or psychological resources needed to transform ourselves. And yet transformation and healing are possible anyway and are offered as pure gift. Jesus breathed out the Spirit on his disciples and continues to breathe out the Spirit on all who are seeking new life today; just as we, even with our spiritual malaise, still love enough to give good gifts to our children, "how much more will the heavenly Father give the Holy Spirit to those who ask him!" (Luke 11:13). Renewal of the heart is there for the asking.

STREAMS OF LIVING WATER

Perhaps we have realized that we do not simply want to say yes to Jesus' invitation to life in the kingdom, we want our lives to become a yes from the inside out. We want to breathe the air of the Spirit, to open our lives to the healing power of God, and allow him to reshape our inner being. How might we go about that? Is there anything we need to do, or do we simply ask for the Spirit, sit back, and wait to be renewed?

There is a beautiful image in the poetry of the Psalms that helpfully illustrates the way God brings this gift of soul healing into our lives. The first psalm opens with these lines:

> Happy are those
> who do not follow the advice of the wicked,
> or take the path that sinners tread,
> or sit in the seat of scoffers;
> but their delight is in the law of the LORD,
> and on his law they meditate day and night.
> They are like trees
> planted by streams of water,
> which yield their fruit in its season,
> and their leaves do not wither.
> In all that they do, they prosper.
>
> The wicked are not so,
> but are like chaff that the wind drives away. (Psalm 1:1-4)

We find ourselves exploring here the distinction between those with a disordered heart and those with a wholly integrated heart. The psalm describes the joy of those who find themselves like trees rooted beside a stream. As the life-giving water soaks into them, they discover they are bearing fruit quite naturally, the spiritual fruit of "love, joy, peace, patience, kindness, generosity, faithfulness, gentleness, and self-control" (Galatians 5:22-23). And this healing of the inner life happens without any effort on their part; they are being transformed from within. A tree makes no conscious decision to grow fruit. It is not by an act of willpower, the result of determination and steely grit, that an apple tree produces apples. The tree simply needs to be located in the right environment: it needs sunlight, water, a temperate climate.

These fruitful trees are contrasted with those who persist in their self-interest and pursuit of pleasure and allow the chaotic disorders of their soul to run rampant, and thus locate themselves far from the living waters of the stream. Unlike the fruitful trees, they become chaff, dried out husks blown around by every breeze: fruitless, rootless, the empty shell of something once living. It's a pitiful image. But it's worth noting that, once again, it's a perfectly natural process. There is no effort involved here; these plants have dried out as the inevitable result of being in the *wrong* environment, one which lacks the water they need.

The implication is that the healing of our souls, which allows us to live well and love deeply, is a gift from beyond ourselves, a process that occurs quite naturally when the living Spirit is allowed to flow through us and animate us from within. But for this to happen the tree needs to be located in the right place, to be rooted in a life-giving environment. And unlike a tree, people are able to make choices that determine the kind of spiritual environment which surrounds them.

The opening of the psalm points toward the nature of these choices. The "happy" or "blessed" people described by the poet have chosen to become immersed in the presence of God as a community (the image used in the Psalms is of people poring over the words of Scripture as a way of listening for God's voice). The psalmist imagines a great fellowship seeking God's presence by soaking themselves in the record of God's presence as experienced throughout the lifetime of the community. And it's here that the broken might become so immersed in the Spirit of God that their twisted loves are straightened out, and they become the "happy" and "blessed" ones who find themselves made whole.

BECOMING LIKE JESUS

The road to healing and transformation described by this psalm is also exactly the way signposted in the Gospels: spiritual practices in community create space for God's renewing of our souls. This is the spirituality of the kingdom. And it's exactly this path that Jesus taught in the Sermon on the Mount, his master class in kingdom living presented in the Gospel of Matthew (chaps. 5-7).

Jesus began by pronouncing a blessing on those who long for purity of heart, who thirst to be loving persons in loving community, but who recognize the poverty of their own spirits (Matthew 5:1-16). He invited his disciples to a life of wholeness, virtue, integrity, meaning, purpose, and direction, which exceeds that experienced by moralizing religious teachers (Matthew 5:17-20). But he showed that the disorders of our hearts underlie our disordered behavior: contempt leads to violence, lust produces marital unfaithfulness, dishonesty causes oath breaking, the holding back of love makes hatred possible (Matthew 5:21-48).

In response to this problem of the heart, Jesus taught some of the basic spiritual practices that create a nurturing environment within which God's Spirit can most fully work to change us: giving to the poor, prayer, fasting, and simplicity—concluding this part of his teaching with an invitation to center our lives on seeking God and seeking God's wholeness, the integrated life that comes as pure gift (Matthew 6:1-34). After warning his disciples to avoid the danger of correcting the faults of others rather than paying attention to their own healing (Matthew 7:1-6), he encouraged them to cultivate the essential receptivity toward God that opens a person's life to the work of the Spirit, telling them to "ask . . . search . . . knock" in expectation of God's willing response (Matthew 7:7-11).

The result of this way of life is the ability to love others fully, and so to fulfill "the law and prophets" (Matthew 7:12). Jesus concluded with an encouragement to choose the right path in life, to look for the growth of fruit rather than deceiving ourselves about our spiritual greatness, to put his teaching into practice (Matthew 7:13-27).

So there is an invitation to life in the kingdom—and a compelling invitation at that: Jesus offers us the possibility of healing, of renewal of the heart, of an end to the destructive disorders of the soul that tear us apart from the inside. God is longing to reshape our hearts; as God said through the prophet Ezekiel some six hundred years before Jesus, "a new heart I will *give* you" (Ezekiel 36:26). But it's an invitation that comes with a profound challenge: we must first confront the reality that we are not kingdom people, that we are not yet people who can love God and others with all our heart and soul. We need to be able to confess that reality to ourselves. And more importantly, we need to learn to confess that reality to one another. That's where it becomes really challenging.

OVER TO YOU

Scripture and Reflection

OVER THE LAST FEW PAGES we've explored the way people responded warmly to Jesus' invitation to life in the kingdom, but also found themselves challenged by the evident need to be loving people themselves in order to live well in a loving community. We've examined the tradition of the "cardinal sins," the mortal sicknesses of the soul that corrupt our essentially loving nature. We've seen how Jesus addressed his invitation precisely to those who struggled with these spiritual maladies and offered healing to those who were willing to immerse themselves in the liberating presence of God.

The following readings and reflection questions might help you consider more fully your own thoughts and responses to these ideas. Again, you might choose to spend a little time each day this week with the suggested passage, or you may prefer to focus in on those reflections that look most helpful.

• *Matthew 21:28-32*

   Why do you think that "tax collectors and prostitutes" found the kingdom message of Jesus so appealing and inviting?

• *Luke 14:25-33*

   Why do you think so many people find the kingdom message of Jesus very challenging and difficult?

- *Joel 2:12–17*

    What do you think are the spiritual roots of your own disordered behavior patterns? What might it mean to "rend your heart, not your clothing" in response to this?

- *James 1:12–16*

    How have you seen the corruption of love at work in your life, progressing through temptation, desire, sin, and heading toward death?

- *Jeremiah 17:5–8*

    How have you experienced processes of spiritual drought or spiritual flourishing in your own life?

- *Ezekiel 36:24–28*

    What does it mean to receive a "new heart" and "new spirit" from God? How do you think that happens?

- *Matthew 6:1–18*

    What are some of the spiritual practices in your life that help draw you into the presence of God? How have they allowed you to experience healing of the soul?

FEARLESS
HONESTY

*We are fearlessly honest
about our weaknesses,
failures, and limits.*

THE TRUTH DEEP WITHIN

PLAY-ACTORS

CONFESSIONS

OVER TO YOU

THE TRUTH
DEEP WITHIN

IT WAS LATE AFTERNOON, the autumn sun filtering weakly through the stained-glass windows, when the young woman walked into church. I'd come over to say Evening Prayer and invited her to join me. She demurred, but asked if I could spare her a few minutes: "I really need to talk with someone," she said. "I'm not religious or anything, but I thought you might be able to help." So we picked out a pew, and I asked her what was on her mind.

She began to unfold a story of painful betrayal and heartache. She'd recently discovered that her partner of many years had been unfaithful to her. The relationship had seemed strong to her, but she'd discovered that he'd been seeing another woman and that the affair had been going on for quite a while. They'd argued, and it had become clear that for some time he'd been cheating on her with a string of different women; their relationship had meant far less to him than she'd believed. He'd left her, and she found herself grieving, bitter, angry, disoriented, and filled with a desperate sorrow.

"It's the anger that's killing me," she told me. "It's been months now since he left, but the anger has stayed with me. It's like poison in my stomach. I can't get rid of it, can't some to terms with it. I've been to see counselors, and they've been helpful, but the anger is still there. I don't know what to do."

I explained to her that I couldn't offer her counseling myself, as I don't have training in that area, but that I'd be happy to refer her to a colleague who might be able to help.

"No," she said, "I don't want to see another counselor. I don't think that'd help."

"Fine," I replied. "Well, here's what I can offer. I'm not a counselor, I'm a priest. I help people to pray. Would that be helpful?"

She thought about it for a moment. "I don't really know if I believe in all that. But I guess it couldn't do any harm. I could give it a try, I suppose."

I thought to myself, *Well, from such mighty seeds of faith, who knows what oaks might grow?* But I kept that to myself and simply answered, "Sounds good to me. Let's start with Prayer 101, a kind of basic introduction. Prayer is simply talking to God. But there's no point in telling God anything that isn't true. So here's my first question: what would be the truth for you right now? How do you really feel about this situation, about this man?"

Her eyes flashed. "I wish he was dead."

I held her fierce gaze. "Well then, that's what you need to pray. Pray for him to die."

PRAYING THE TRUTH

The young woman was startled. This clearly wasn't what she'd expected to hear either. "I can't do that!" she said.

"What else are you going to do?" I replied. "Sugarcoat a lie? Do you think God doesn't already know how you feel, what's going on in your life? There's no point telling anything other than the truth."

She looked deeply skeptical. "I'm not doing that," she insisted.

I decided to try a different tack. "I understand it's difficult. Here's another idea. Would you be willing to pray a prayer written by God?"

"I suppose so," she answered uncertainly.

I picked up a Bible from the pew and opened up the book of Psalms. "This is a collection of prayers right in the middle of the Bible," I told her. "And the Bible was written by God, right?" (This wasn't the time or place for a philosophical exploration of the nature of Scripture.) "So these must be good prayers, with the divine seal of approval. You can't go wrong praying one of these, can you?"

"Sure," she replied, "why not?"

"Well, here's the prayer I want you to use." I took a pen and circled these verses from Psalm 55:

> It is not my enemies who taunt me—
>> I could bear that;
> it is not adversaries who deal insolently with me—
>> I could hide from them.
> But it is you, my equal,
>> my companion, my familiar friend,
> with whom I kept pleasant company;
>> we walked in the house of God with the throng.
> Let death come upon them;
>> let them go down alive to Sheol;
>> for evil is in their homes and in their hearts.
>> (Psalm 55:12-15)

"It's a prayer asking that a betrayer might die," I told her. "It's *your* prayer, the true prayer of your heart. I want you to take this Bible home and pray this prayer every day."

She took the Bible from me, somewhat unsure, but agreed to do as I'd asked.

FINDING A NEW TRUTH

A few weeks later we saw one another again. I asked her if she had been using the psalm to pray. She told me she had.

"Have you noticed any result?" I asked her.

"He's not dead yet!" she replied with a surprising vehemence.

But I refused to be discouraged. "Keep going," I urged her. "Keep praying."

Some weeks later we met again—the last time I ever saw her. Once more I asked her if she was still using the prayer.

"Not every day," she replied. I asked her why not. "Well, you said I was *never* to pray anything that wasn't true!" she said in an accusatory tone. "And one day I found myself looking down at those words, and they just weren't true anymore. At least, not that day. I'm still hurting. But I realized I didn't want him to die."

"So what did you do then?" I asked.

"I looked through some of the other prayers in the book," she answered, "and found one that seemed more suitable. I've been using that one. I hope you don't mind."

THE HONESTY OF BIBLICAL PRAYER

That young woman was shocked and surprised when I suggested that she pray for her former partner to die. I've told this story in many contexts since that day, and wherever I tell it people seem equally startled at the advice I offered. Which raises a simple and straightforward question: *what should she have prayed?* It sounds marvelously pious to say that she should have prayed for grace to love him, for mercy and forgiveness, for a change in her own heart so she could come to terms with his behavior. And these would have been good things to pray. But they wouldn't have been *true*.

If we learn anything from the school of prayer we find in the book of Psalms, often described as the "prayer book of the Bible," it's that honesty is everything. The poets who wrote these ancient prayers were unafraid to expose their hearts to God and to the community, creating songs filled with joy, wonder, celebration, pageantry, satisfaction, gentleness, peace, and more—but also with rage, horror, lament, darkness, doubt, shock, and despair. Nothing was held back. At times the poetry is upbeat and uplifting:

Let everything that breathes praise the LORD!
Praise the LORD! (Psalm 150:6)

O give thanks to the Lord, for he is good,
    for his steadfast love endures forever. (Psalm 136:1)

My soul is satisfied as with a rich feast,
    and my mouth praises you with joyful lips. (Psalm 63:5)

Make a joyful noise to the Lord, all the earth.
    Worship the Lord with gladness;
    come into his presence with singing. (Psalm 100:1-2)

But there are a myriad of other voices in these pages, many of them difficult and uncomfortable:

O Lord, why do you cast me off?
    Why do you hide your face from me? (Psalm 88:14)

How long, O God, is the foe to scoff?
    Is the enemy to revile your name forever?
Why do you hold back your hand;
    why do you keep your hand in your bosom? (Psalm 74:10-11)

O Lord, heal me, for my bones are shaking with terror.
My soul also is struck with terror,
    while you, O Lord—how long? (Psalm 6:2-3)

Contend, O Lord, with those who contend with me;
    fight against those who fight against me! (Psalm 35:1)

Do I not hate those who hate you, O Lord?
    And do I not loathe those who rise up against you?
I hate them with perfect hatred;
    I count them my enemies. (Psalm 139:21-22)

Alongside the soaring hallelujahs and angelic cries of praise we hear the most vulnerable, sorrowful, sometimes spiteful, and occasionally downright vicious words. Psalm 108 opens with a beautiful morning chorus of worship:

> My heart is steadfast, O God, my heart is steadfast;
>> I will sing and make melody.
>> Awake, my soul!
> Awake, O harp and lyre!
>> I will awake the dawn. (Psalm 108:1-2)

But in the very next psalm, the poet vents his spleen against an unnamed foe in an extended outburst of the most astonishing and malicious cursing in the whole Bible:

> May his days be few;
>> may another seize his position.
> May his children be orphans,
>> and his wife a widow. . . .
> He clothed himself with cursing as his coat,
>> may it soak into his body like water,
>> like oil into his bones. (Psalm 109:8-9, 18)

And this is just a sampling of the writer's anger; the whole wretched curse stretches across some thirty lines of bitterness and bile.

It's unpleasant reading. But it's also a brutally honest insight into the broken and disordered human heart. If we have not experienced these depths of emotion, it may only be because we've never found ourselves in the circumstances that would provoke them. This is the shadow side of human nature speaking aloud; this is the darkness each of us carries within. We are all bearers of scars and pain; we are all twisted and confused; we are all rebellious and self-centered. We know that in the Gospels Jesus invites us to a life of love, but we have also learned to spurn, to spit, to hate. There is a reason Jesus has to say "love your enemies": because we all *have* enemies. It is precisely when our hearts want to tell us that we're not that bad, that we're good people really, that the psalmist's fire and fury is not found in us—precisely then that the words of Jeremiah need to ring in our ears:

> The heart is devious above all else;
>> it is perverse—
>> who can understand it? (Jeremiah 17:9)

PLAY-ACTORS

In his announcement of the good news about the kingdom of God, Jesus combined a deep understanding of the grace, mercy, and forgiveness of God with an open-eyed realism about the depravity of human nature. He held out a vision of a loving community centered on God, and invited people to come and share in the realization of that vision. But he also recognized that the darkness that people experience from without (and so often choose to embrace from within) is pervasive and destructive, and needs to be faced squarely.

Jesus spoke particularly strongly to those who behaved as "hypocrites." The Greek word used in the Gospels describes stage actors, a profession considered to be rather disreputable in the first century. Hypocrites, to Jesus' contemporaries, were people who pretended to be something other than they really were; they assumed masks, faces, opinions, and emotions not their own. The behavior and words they exhibited on the stage came not from the heart and soul but from the writer's script. These play-actors lacked authenticity and integrity. They were sham people.

It was this accusation that Jesus leveled at many of the religious leaders of his day. "Woe to you, scribes and Pharisees, hypocrites!" he cried out repeatedly on one occasion reported in Matthew's Gospel.

> You lock people out of the kingdom of heaven. . . . You tithe mint, dill, and cummin, and have neglected the weightier matters of the law: justice and mercy and faith. . . . You clean the outside of

> the cup and of the plate, but inside they are full of greed and
> self-indulgence. . . . You are like whitewashed tombs, which on
> the outside look beautiful, but inside they are full of the bones of
> the dead and of all kinds of filth. (Matthew 23:13-14, 23, 25, 27)

The imagery makes his point crystal clear: the problem was not that they did wrong but that they covered their wrongdoing and pretended to be so righteous. By keeping up a pretense of holiness, they ended up simply playing at life, acting a part as though it were true (in Shakespeare's phrase) that "all the world's a stage, and all the men and women merely players."

The real issue, as Jesus saw it, was not maintaining a meticulous obedience to the finer points of the biblical law, but rather facing the deep problems of the human soul that those laws sought to address. The Pharisees and scribes confronted Jesus once about his disciples' failure to perform the careful ritual washing of their hands that should precede a meal. In response, Jesus challenged them on two fronts.

First, he criticized them for setting aside the clear teaching of Scripture in order to maintain traditions developed over the centuries in response to the texts. Although these verbal teachings had emerged to clarify what obedience to the law might look like in different practical contexts, Jesus suggested that it was nonsensical to use them to *replace* the Scripture's obvious intent. So, for example, the Hebrew Scriptures describe sacrifices offered to God as *corban*, and the tradition developed that anything intentionally set aside to be devoted to God could also be considered *corban*. Clearly, once it had been so designated it would be inappropriate to allow it to be taken back for any other use. But while such a designation makes sense most of the time, it appears it was being abused by the first century to allow people to avoid giving support to their aging parents. "You say that if anyone tells father or mother, 'Whatever support you might have had from me is Corban' (that is, an offering to God)—then you no longer permit doing anything for a father or mother, thus making void the word of God through your tradition" (Mark 7:11-13). Different aspects of Moses' teaching were being played against one another in ways that entirely missed the spirit of the Bible.

THE HEART OF THE PROBLEM

Behind this lay an even more serious problem: the inability to understand the very purpose of Scripture. It was here that Jesus turned his attention next. "Listen to me, all of you, and understand," he called out, drawing the wider crowd into his conversation. "There is nothing outside a person that by going in can defile, but the things that come out are what defile" (Mark 7:14-15). Jesus was making the startling assertion that, *kosher* practice notwithstanding, all foods could be considered clean. "Whatever goes into a person from outside cannot defile," he clarified rather graphically, "since it enters, not the heart but the stomach, and goes out into the sewer" (Mark 7:18-19).

The root human problem lies not with clean and unclean foods, Jesus insisted, but with the heart. And he saw that the sickness of the heart was deeply entrenched and far-reaching in its scope. "It is from within," he said, "from the human heart, that evil intentions come: fornication, theft, murder, adultery, avarice, wickedness, deceit, licentiousness, envy, slander, pride, folly. All these evil things come from within, and they defile a person" (Mark 7:21-23). It's a candid roster of depravity reminiscent of the list of cardinal sins we encountered in the chapter titled "Love in Everything." This is what lurks, in some form or another, in the darkness of our hearts; for each of us, some form of this "sin is lurking at the door" (Genesis 4:7), as God warned Cain. To deny this—especially while playing religious games intended to present us to the world as untainted and pure—is to live the great lie of the hypocrite.

Twelve-step groups (such as Alcoholics Anonymous), in the first few steps of their program, encourage members to recognize that they are confronted by problems too overwhelming to solve by themselves, to seek the power of God in their lives to bring healing to those problems, and then to make a "searching and fearless moral inventory" with the aim of admitting those wrongs to God and making amends to others for the damage brought into their lives through wayward behavior.

There is a deep spiritual wisdom at work here. As long as we continue to try to hide our brokenness from ourselves, from others, and from God, we cannot expect any serious change or healing in our lives. We're simply play-acting at life, wearing masks to hide our weaknesses and shortcomings while failing to face the root issues that are slowly destroying us from within like a cancer of the soul. Making a searching inventory of our moral lives is painful. It's never easy for any of us to face our shadows, the darkness that haunts us from deep within our hearts. It also means facing the guilt and shame that darkness brings to birth, and accepting our responsibility for the continued power of that darkness over our life and relationships. Opening and cleaning our spiritual wounds requires enormous courage.

One of those powerfully honest psalmists had once written: "You desire truth in the inward being" (Psalm 51:6), and Jesus was constantly looking for those willing to face their own inward truth. Peter first realized that Jesus was no ordinary Jewish rabbi when Jesus led him to a miraculous catch of hundreds of fish. Peter responded by falling to his knees and saying, "Go away from me, Lord, for I am a sinful man!" But Jesus responded not to his unrighteousness but to his honesty and openness of heart. "Do not be afraid," he replied; "from now on you will be catching people" (Luke 5:1-11).

The woman who came to the home of Simon the Pharisee had a similar experience. As she bathed Jesus' feet in her penitent tears, she knew she had made serious mistakes, knew her inner self to be damaged and misaligned. Jesus responded to her warmly: "Your sins are forgiven" (Luke 7:48).

We might also remember that as Jesus was dying nailed to a cross the thief crucified alongside acknowledged his own wrongdoing, and in an expression of trust in God's mercy asked, "Jesus, remember me when you come into your kingdom." Without a hint of condemnation Jesus warmly accepted the man's open heart. "Truly I tell you," he answered, "today you will be with me in Paradise" (Luke 23:39-43).

IN THE HANDS OF AN ANGRY GOD?

"It is a fearful thing to fall into the hands of the living God," says the seventeenth-century Anglican Book of Common Prayer in a service titled "A Commination, or Denouncing of God's Anger and Judgements Against Sinners." "He shall pour down rain upon the sinners," it continues, "snares, fire and brimstone, storm and tempest; this shall be their portion to drink." The sermon at the heart of the service stitches together some of the most challenging and (frankly) unpleasant passages of the Bible into a fierce tirade against all that is evil in the world and those who inhabit it, and couches the whole in a warning of dire punishments soon to come from the hand of God. "Then shall appear the wrath of God in the day of vengeance, which obstinate sinners, through the stubbornness of their hearts, have heaped upon themselves; which despised the goodness, patience, and long-sufferance of God, when he calleth them continually to repentance." The whole liturgy is designed to reduce us, "who are vile earth, and miserable sinners," to abject submission on our knees. The language is strong and stirring, and hearing the service must have been a powerful experience. But it's not an experience many have shared in our day. In twenty years as a priest in the Anglican Church I've never heard the service used once.

Perhaps that's just as well. It's not a liturgy that reflects well the tenor of Jesus' teaching about confession and repentance. Although Jesus could break out in eloquent anger at times, notably against the play-acting of the hypocritical religious leaders discussed earlier, his approach to those whose lives were broken and disordered by poor choices and unloving behavior was more typically conciliatory and sympathetic, not dwelling on their mistakes but encouraging them to acknowledge their wrongdoing, to open themselves to God's merciful forgiveness, and to begin again. Jesus was less of a hellfire preacher and more a healing physician.

OR IN THE HANDS OF MERCY?

In fact, it was in exactly those terms—as a healing physician—that he defended himself when challenged by the scribes and Pharisees about freely associating with the most troubled and reviled members of his society: the "tax collectors and sinners" (Luke 5:30). In Roman Palestine the tax collectors were collaborators who helped finance the hated occupying powers through revenue raising, frequently defrauding people in the process in order to feather their own nests. They were seen as traitors, betraying their own nation and people for sordid financial gain. "Sinners" was a wide category of moral reprobates who were assumed to keep company with the tax collectors: crooks and thugs, sharp dealers and swindlers, and women of loose moral character. They were not the people with whom a respectable rabbi should be enjoying easy company, let alone allowing them to be part of his group of disciples.

But Jesus called Levi the tax collector to join his inner circle of apprentices. He accepted an invitation to a banquet at Levi's home. He sat at table with the sinners and reprobates. The religious leaders, scandalized, were unwilling to confront Jesus directly, but complained to his followers: "Why do you eat and drink with tax collectors and sinners?" Jesus, overhearing, answered with characteristic directness: "Those who are well have no need of a physician, but those who are sick; I have come to call not the righteous but sinners to repentance" (Luke 5:27-32).

For Jesus, this was the purpose of drawing people to a truthful acknowledgment of their interior brokenness. Not to conjure up the kind of self-loathing and recrimination that fuels an excess of guilt. And not as a prelude to indulging in furious denunciations of moral laxity seasoned with promises of divine retribution. Jesus sought honesty about the heart the way any doctor would seek honesty from a patient: in order to bring the true nature of a condition into the open, to uncover the full range of symptoms and underlying causes, and to take the first steps toward healing and wholeness.

CONFESSIONS

CONFESSION. For some it conjures up the image of a penitent kneeling beside a mesh screen, quietly murmuring a litany of sins to the priest half-hidden in the shadows. To others, it might suggest the awkward revelation of our indiscretions to a friend, a spouse, or a lover. Some, perhaps, would think of difficult conversations at work as we explain the shortcomings in our management of time and resources, our failure to complete a given task.

Whatever the circumstances, for most of us confession is a painful business: bringing into the light our foolishness, our failures, our weaknesses—or worse, having to own up to the darkness within, the twisted desires in our hearts that drive our most shameful and problematic behavior. And many people find this kind of honesty so difficult they can never truly bring themselves to confess anything.

NEVER KNOWINGLY WRONG

I can vividly remember a conversation I had once with Alice, a member of one of my churches with a very short temper and liable to fly off the handle at the slightest provocation. One Sunday she'd lashed out at one of the youngsters in church and threatened to hit the child; I went to see her the next morning to talk it through and ensure she understood that her behavior had been unacceptable. It quickly turned into a nose-to-nose standup argument. She simply refused to accept any responsibility for her actions. The child was at fault, she told me, for being noisy. I was at fault for not stopping the noise. The congregation were to blame, and her neighbors; her husband carried the blame, together with the lay ministers and the organist. She blamed her parents, her doctor, the bishop, and everyone else who came to mind. It was *everyone's* fault—except hers. She found the simple act of confession impossible: it would have hurt her too much, she seemed to think, to accept responsibility and own up to doing wrong.

Rightly understood, though, the act of confession (to God and to one another) is not something to be feared: an exercise in self-flagellation or a morose wallowing in guilt. In reality it's a gift, an opportunity finally to come into the open. Genesis describes the outcome of the first turning away from God and from the community of love: Adam conceals himself in the undergrowth and tells the Lord, "I heard the sound of you in the garden, and I was afraid, because I was naked; and I hid myself" (Genesis 3:10). When we confess the truth about ourselves we come out of hiding and accept our moral nakedness. And that's difficult and uncomfortable, but it's also the essential first step toward being reconciled with God, receiving mercy, and experiencing the healing grace of the Holy Spirit.

FROM THE DEPTHS OF MERCY

Our confidence in making our confession can only come from a profound appreciation of the mercy and love of God for us: we have to *know* in the depths of our soul that God is *for* us—and, as the apostle Paul asks: "If God is for us, who is against us? He who did not withhold his own Son, but gave him up for all of us, will he not with him also give us everything else? Who will bring any charge against God's elect? It is God who justifies. Who is to condemn?" (Romans 8:31-34).

Many of us struggle with a tremendously negative view of God, gleaned perhaps from moralizing sermons heard in church, from artistic images portraying God as a distant and stern figure, even from lazy cultural caricatures of religion as nothing more than judgmentalism dressed in pious language. Combined with the lack of self-worth so many people seem to suffer, we come to assume that God sees us the way the imaginary God of popular culture *would* see a person with the troubles and darkness we know lurk within us. And so, in my experience, many people picture God as a fierce judge, or a distant and disinterested cosmic engineer, or a frustrated parent wrestling with a disappointing child.

Perhaps that's why Jesus' teaching about God was so astonishing to his first hearers—and can be to us, when we set aside our overfamiliarity with many of the Gospel stories and hear them again afresh. God, said Jesus, is like a shepherd who abandons the care of his considerable flock of sheep to cross dangerous territory in order to find one lost lamb (Luke 15:3-7). He is like a heartbroken father who scans the horizon for the return of his wayward son, and launches a mighty celebration when he sees him appear at the end of the road (Luke 15:11-24). He showers his grace wherever and whenever he chooses, often to the surprise of those who thought they had cornered the market on God (Matthew 20:1-16). He even gives the kingdom of heaven to children, who have done nothing to deserve it (Matthew 19:14). Jesus compared God to a man throwing a tremendous wedding party who refuses to be discouraged when the expected guests fail to turn up and sends his slaves out to draw in whoever will respond: "Those slaves went out into the streets," Jesus said, "and gathered all whom they found, both good and bad; so the wedding hall was filled with guests" (Matthew 22:10). God's mercy is boundless, his compassion endless, his love eternal and irrepressible; he is

> The LORD, the LORD,
> a God merciful and gracious,
> slow to anger,
> and abounding in steadfast love and faithfulness,
> keeping steadfast love for the thousandth generation,
> forgiving iniquity and transgression and sin. (Exodus 34:6-7)

No wonder, then, that Jesus asserted with such confidence to Nicodemus: "Indeed, God did not send the Son into the world to condemn the world, but in order that the world might be saved through him" (John 3:17).

The old Book of Common Prayer, for all its magnificence of language and depth of spirituality (and I write as someone who prays with it daily), missed the mark in its "Commination" service. For all that God *is* angered by our wrongdoing, which after all is not without consequence and can wreak such devastation in our own lives and the lives of others, Jesus never spoke of God as a furious parent needing to be placated before his irritation burst forth in judgment. He spoke of a loving Father, a merciful Creator, a gracious God who seeks and rescues the lost, who embraces the returning wanderer, and who heals the broken. The God to whom we confess in naked honesty already knows our innermost self better than we know it ourselves—and with passionate longing he urges us to come home.

CREATING A CULTURE OF VULNERABILITY

Confession, they say, is good for the soul; it's also good for a community. The same openness and vulnerability we are encouraged to show toward God can also help to create deeper and healthier relationships with one another. In the New Testament letter of James, the writer encourages the community of Christ-followers to "confess your sins to one another, and pray for one another, so that you may be healed" (James 5:16). Over the centuries this became a very formalized transaction: private confession to a priest followed by a liturgical pronouncement of absolution. And this certainly can have great value for many; I know from my own experience how the words of forgiveness spoken by a priest in the name of God can unlock years of struggle with guilt and unforgiveness in some people's hearts.

But the letter of James seems to have in mind here not so much a ritualized exchange but more a culture of trust and care, which makes it possible for people to be honest about their failings and moral weaknesses. Again, twelve-step groups provide a great example of this working well: the climate of confidence and nonjudgment they create and cherish allows people to admit to deep-seated problems and issues, knowing they will receive nothing but support and care in return. These communities attract people whose moral lives are often severely compromised, but the community's purpose is not to censure people for their failures or to pontificate about moral absolutes: their purpose is *recovery*. So people are encouraged to be very open and vulnerable about their addictions, their failings, their struggles, and their brokenness as their first step toward wholeness.

Honesty like this depends on a mutual trust, which can only be nurtured slowly and which is easily broken. A community seeking this degree of healing confession has to commit itself to a degree of confidentiality and nonjudgment that many people seem to find hard to maintain—perhaps that's why communities characterized by such vulnerability are so rare and so sought after. In a culture where we all long simply to "be ourselves," we can be surprisingly reluctant to accept others as they truly are.

But the problem is hardly unique to our age. Reading the apostle Paul's letters to Corinth, we find that one of the members had been committing some scandalous sin that was causing widespread offense. Paul wrote in strong terms urging them to deal with the situation before the moral laxity in their midst infected the whole community: "drive out the wicked person from among you" (1 Corinthians 5:13). But in his next letter we discover that the person they had excluded had repented of his wrongdoing and asked for his relationship with the community to be restored—only to find himself stonewalled, pushed away, shunned.

The Egyptian desert monk Anthony the Great was faced with a similar situation a few centuries later. One of the monks had committed some unspeakable sin, but later repented and tried to return to his community, only to be spurned. Anthony's message to the community was both firm and compassionate: "A ship was lost in the ocean and lost its cargo, and with great difficulty the empty ship was brought to land. Do you want to run the ship that has been rescued onto the rocks and sink it?"

Paul's response was similar. "The punishment by the majority is enough; . . . so now instead you should forgive and console him, so that he may not be overwhelmed by excessive sorrow. So I urge you to reaffirm your love for him" (2 Corinthians 2:6-8). Like us, they found it easier to judge than forgive, easier to exclude than reconcile, easier to see the speck in another's eye than to see the log in their own (Matthew 7:4).

We are not called to be the ethical guardians of society, but rather a haven for the morally broken and compromised. And for that we don't need platitudes and certainties, we need tender hearts and for-giving souls. In a world of judgment we are to be a people of mercy. We openly accept our weakness, our inability to be who we should be. It is a difficult position to take in a world where power, strength, and force are so respected and valued. But in the end it is the only place from which healing can possibly begin.

OVER TO YOU

Scripture and Reflection

OVER THESE LAST FEW PAGES we've reflected on the need for honesty in our relationships with God and one another. We've looked at the radical and sometimes shocking honesty exhibited by the book of Psalms as a model for our own prayer. We've seen the contempt that Jesus held for hypocrisy and play-acting, contrasted with the great value he placed on openness and truth about our moral weaknesses. We've seen how Jesus encouraged honesty and vulnerability as a first step toward reconciliation and healing. And we've considered what it might mean to try to create that degree of openness in the communities we belong to.

The following readings and reflection questions could stimulate your own thinking and prayer about honesty with God and one another. Again, you may find it more helpful to tackle a handful of the questions individually. Or, if you prefer, you may be helped by working through each reading on a daily basis over this next week.

- *Jonah 4:1-8*

  How do you pray your most difficult emotions: anger, bitterness, hatred, disappointment, betrayal, sadness?

- *Psalm 88*

  How comfortable are you with sharing your sorrows and darkness with God and others? What would help you be more open?

- *Psalm 137*

    How do you find yourself responding to this difficult prayer? What prompted the poet to pray in this way? How easy or difficult is it to pray with this degree of honesty?

- *James 5:13-18*

    What has been your experience of confessing to others? What was helpful about it? What was difficult or unhelpful?

- *Acts 15:36-41*

    How do we decide when to exercise discipline in our communities and when to exercise forgiveness?

- *Daniel 9:4-10*

    What do you find helpful in Daniel's approach to confession in this prayer? What is difficult or challenging?

- *Matthew 5:21-26*

    Are there issues you need to resolve with someone else before reading any further in this book?

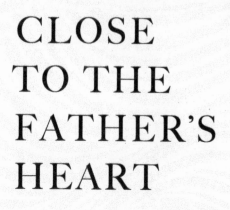

CLOSE TO THE FATHER'S HEART

*We long to experience God
in silence, prayer, and Scripture.*

LONGING OF THE HEART

INTIMACY AND SEPARATION

THE JOURNEY INTO GOD

OVER TO YOU

LONGING OF
THE HEART

A FEW YEARS AGO FIVE MEN WALKED through the doors of an English monastery to film one of the strangest and most surprising reality TV shows of our time. *The Monastery*, first screened later that year, told the story of their forty days spent in the silence, prayer, and reflection with the monks of Worth Abbey—and the transformations they experienced along the way.

Toward the end of the third show viewers were treated to a remarkably profound few minutes of television. One of the five men, Tony, had been touched very deeply by his time in the abbey, and as the forty days drew to a close he became quite agitated about the prospect of returning to his everyday life. After a chaotic few years of alcohol and drug abuse, he'd come close to taking his own life. After a period of recovery and rehabilitation he'd found his feet a little, but was still struggling to hold himself together; immediately before spending time in the monastery he'd spent time as a freelance employee for a soft-porn TV channel working alongside "some of the most unpleasant men I'd ever had the misfortune to meet." The prospect of going back, after more than a month of quiet and stability, was distressing.

Tony brought this to his last meeting with Brother Francis, his spiritual guide in the community. The two men sat facing each other in a small sitting room. Tony explained that he couldn't simply give up his work, however much he might dislike it; after all, he said, he had to earn money to pay the rent and put food on the table.

Brother Francis encouraged him to stop thinking about the demands of the next few days and instead to become aware of wider horizons. "Vocation's about discovering who you really are," he said, "and what you should really be doing." He gave Tony a gift, a small white stone, and explained that the book of Revelation describes Christ giving people a white stone that has written on it "a new name that no one knows except the one who receives it" (Revelation 2:17). "I think our vocation is to find out what that name is," Brother Francis continued. "And I think that's a lifelong quest."

Tony, taking the gift, sat back. "I do really feel confused by this whole thing," he replied. "It's easy to try to verbalize the whole thing—for the sake of wrapping it up in words, you know?"

Brother Francis interrupted him. "I wouldn't bother. I wouldn't bother."

And then a deep silence fell between them. A silence that stretched on and on. The quiet stillness they shared seemed pregnant with the presence of God, a presence that could be sensed even through the cold glass of the TV screen.

Finally, Tony said quietly, "I feel quite odd."

Reflecting on those few minutes afterwards, Tony told the camera, "That's the weirdest experience I've ever had in my whole life. It was a religious experience." And speaking about it some years later he described "a feeling of lightheadedness and paralysis—a surge of emotion which reduced me to tears and a knowledge that whatever I had been trying to contact or access had replied or at least let me in."

Tony had been touched by God. And it profoundly changed his life.

DIVINE HOMESICKNESS

The deepest yearning of our human hearts, whether we recognize it or not, is for this experience of intimacy with God. "For God alone my soul waits in silence," writes one of the psalmists, opening one of the many poems at the heart of the Bible that speak of this longing for divine intimacy (Psalm 62:1). The next psalm in the collection begins with a cry of anguish:

> O God, you are my God, I seek you,
>   my soul thirsts for you;
> my flesh faints for you,
>   as in a dry and weary land where there is no water.
>   (Psalm 63:1)

The late-sixteenth-century Anglican priest William Morgan, when translating the Bible into Welsh, used a passionate and evocative word in the third line of this psalm to capture this sense of yearning: *hiraeth*. (To pronounce the word, imagine adding the sound at the middle of "python"—without the *p* and *on*—to the English word *here*: the result would be something like "here-ayth.") "*Hiraethodd fy nghnawd am-danat*," he wrote, which might literally be rendered as "my body is homesick for you."

Hiraeth is a powerful and emotionally dense word in Welsh (in some ways similar to *sehnsucht* in German or *saudade* in Portuguese); it's almost impossible to translate the emotional content of the word into English. Being homesick can mean a longing for our country, our hometown, or simply the place we happen to be living at the moment. It speaks of the desire to return to familiarity. But *hiraeth* uniquely describes the yearning felt by those away from the place of their birth and nurture, those who are separated from the towns and villages, the hills and rivers, where they walked and played and wept as child and adult. It is a longing for the stories, the songs, the familiar faces that have shaped our entire lives. *Hiraeth* speaks to the heart's longing for its one true home.

And with this word Morgan sought to capture our sense of longing for God: a yearning for the heart's true home in the presence of the Father. This is not a desire for any earthly place; nor is it a hunger for heaven—at least, if we understand heaven as a kind of geographical place we go to when we die. Our hearts hunger for the presence of God, and nothing else in this world or the next can even begin to satisfy that hunger. We burn with a passionate desire that cannot be answered by anything other than divine intimacy. We are a people of holy *hiraeth*.

This homesickness, a deep-seated yearning for intimacy with God, characterized the life, teaching, and activity of Jesus from the very beginning. In fact, that's where John's Gospel begins, not with the story of Jesus' birth (where Matthew and Luke open the narrative) or his appearance as a teacher in Palestine (as in Mark) but with Jesus, before all time, dwelling from eternity in the presence of his Father. "In the beginning was the Word," John writes of Christ in his famous opening line, "and the Word was with God, and the Word was God" (John 1:1). A few paragraphs later John expands on what it means for Jesus to be "with God": "No one has ever seen God. It is God the only Son, who is close to the Father's heart, who has made him known" (John 1:18).

CLOSE TO THE FATHER'S HEART

John's image here draws on the cultural experience of ancient peoples sharing a meal together. In Jesus' time guests at dinner didn't sit on straight-backed chairs separated by comfortable elbow room as we do today; they would recline around a low table, leaning on one arm, lying up against one another like sardines in a can. The feet of the guest to your left would be close at your back, which was one of the many good reasons people washed their feet before eating together. And the guest to your right, the position of honor, would be lying close enough simply to lean back against your chest for a quiet, private conversation. And this is how John imagines the divine fellowship of God: Father and Son reclining at table, Jesus resting his head "close to the Father's heart," where he can listen to the Father's heartbeat and hear the softest whisper of his voice. It's a picture of extraordinary tenderness and affection.

But we are not simply observers of this beautiful intimacy; over and again in John's Gospel Jesus extends an invitation to dwell with him, to recline "close to the Father's heart." It's an invitation offered to the inner circle of apostles, to the wider community of Christ's disciples, and to John's readers—that is, to us.

In the tenth chapter of the Gospel, for example, Jesus compared his relationship with his followers to that of a shepherd with his sheep, a relationship characterized by familiarity, trust, and obedience. "The sheep follow him because they know his voice," he said (John 10:4). He reminded them that a loyal shepherd will defend the sheep even at the cost of his own life. But then he pushed beyond this homely, rural metaphor to describe the astonishing closeness those who follow him might experience: "I know my own and my own know me, *just as the Father knows me and I know the Father*" (John 10:14-15, emphasis added). This far exceeds the relationship between a herdsman and his livestock; Jesus was offering to draw those who respond to his voice into the same kind of heart-to-heart intimacy that he already enjoyed with his heavenly Father.

A few chapters later, while talking with his disciples in the upper room on the night before his death, Jesus spoke about this intimacy even more explicitly. He had openly predicted his imminent betrayal and death; the shadow of death was already hanging over the room, and the disciples had every reason to be anxious about what the dawning of the following day might bring. So Jesus sought to reassure them. "Do not let your hearts be troubled," he counseled them (John 14:1). He encouraged them to trust in God and in himself, and to have faith that the action he was about to undertake would prepare a place for them. "I will come again and will take you to myself," he concluded, "so that where I am, there you may be also" (John 14:3). His followers were confused by this at first, and many of John's later readers have shared that confusion: is this a promise of supernatural dwellings in heaven, of mansions beyond the sky? But John, of course, intends us to understand no such thing; he has already clearly shown us where Jesus dwells: "close to the Father's heart." Jesus wasn't offering to scoop up his followers into a distant spiritual realm. He was intending to lead them into the Father's embrace, right here and now.

DWELLING IN THE FATHER

That same theme is echoed in the following chapter in Jesus' famous image of the vine and vinedresser. "I am the true vine. . . . Just as the branch cannot bear fruit by itself unless it abides in the vine, neither can you unless you abide in me" (John 15:1, 4). The disciples might well have wondered what "abiding" in Jesus could possibly mean; the ambiguity and uncertainty are deliberate, as elsewhere in John's Gospel, and intended to make the hearer (or reader) reflect more deeply. As he continued to develop his theme Jesus began to open up the imagery: "If you abide in me, and my words abide in you, ask for whatever you wish, and it will be done for you" (John 15:7). There is a magnificent generosity in that offer which is consistent with the proclamation of the kingdom as a gift of God's grace. After all, if life itself and all creation are sheer gift, what would God now choose to hold back from us? But it is the opening words that should truly astonish us, the suggestion that by allowing Jesus' words to abide in us we might somehow find ourselves abiding in him. Not simply hearing him, seeing him, receiving revelations of his will, but dwelling in his intimate presence; as Jesus phrased it a few sentences later, "you will abide in my love, just as I have kept my Father's commandments and abide in his love" (John 15:10). Once again we find ourselves being drawn into the same circle of relationship Jesus already enjoys with the Father.

Perhaps most striking, however, is the opening of Jesus' prayer for the disciples in the seventeenth chapter. "Father, the hour has come," he said, referring to his impending crucifixion; "glorify your Son so that the Son may glorify you" (John 17:1). Throughout the Gospel the motif of *glorifying* (often linked with *lifting up*) is repeatedly used to point toward the cross and Jesus' offering of his own life to bring life to others; it is in this act of supreme obedience to the Father and love for the world that his glory is most fully revealed (see John 7:39; 12:16; 12:27-32; 13:31-33). And the giving of his life brings *eternal life* (another recurring motif) to others; the giving of this life is Jesus' purpose in coming from heaven to earth (see John 3:16; 5:24; 6:40; 10:10). But eternal life is not simply an existence that never comes to an end—which could, of course, be unendurably bland or an unceasing torture. It is a quality of life rather than a quantity of years; eternal life is the life in abundance Jesus offered to those who recognized his voice and came to share with him the relationship he enjoyed with the Father (John 10:10). And this is precisely the nature of eternal life as Jesus describes it in the next words of his prayer: "This is eternal life, that they may know you, the only true God, and Jesus Christ whom you have sent" (John 17:3).

Scholars have often noted that, just as John interprets the Gospel story for his Gentile readers by replacing Jewish concepts like "Messiah" with more familiar philosophical terms such as the "Logos," the universal creative principle (John 1:1-18), so he seems to use "eternal life" as a substitute for the Hebraic idea of the "kingdom of God." If this understanding of John's Gospel is correct, then in Jesus' prayer (read in the light of the rest of John) we find the kingdom of God being identified with an eternal, abundant life whose essential nature is this: life lived in intimate relationship with the Father through Jesus Christ.

We are back in the territory of the kingdom of God that so fills the other three Gospels. A community of love in which life is shared with countless others. A community of broken people needing and seeking transformation. A profoundly God-soaked community, a community of divine intimacy. A people gathered at table with the Lord, where we find that everyone is offered the opportunity to lean back into the Father's embrace, to hear his whisper, and to listen to his heartbeat. And this place of intimacy is, in the end, our true home: it is the place for which our souls long, for which we thirst and hunger with every fiber of our being. Our yearning for the Father's heart is our holy *hiraeth*.

INTIMACY AND
SEPARATION

WE DON'T ALWAYS EXPERIENCE this closeness and intimacy, of course. According to surveys a great many people (whether Christian or not, religious or agnostic or even atheist) claim to have had spiritual and religious experiences, the sense of touching a reality beyond themselves. In one survey, conducted in the United Kingdom in 2000, 75 percent of respondents claimed to be "aware of a spiritual dimension to their experience," while numerous researchers in the United Kingdom and United States have found that around half the population will report having had at least one "religious or mystical experience" in their lives. Perhaps sensing the presence of God isn't as unusual as we might think.

But God doesn't always seem near at hand, even for those who are particularly devout or mystically inclined. And this seeming absence of God may not be linked in an obvious way to our own behavior; it's not invariably a result of our turning away from him. I once came across a sign outside a church: "If God seems far away, guess who moved?" But those kinds of simplistic questions aren't always helpful when God's presence is hard to discern. I've known people in illness, in depression, in stressful circumstances, or simply going through deep periods of growth in their life of prayer who have lived, sometimes for years, with a deep sense of God's absence (even while they held firmly to the belief that this God, who seemed so distant, was always with them). We keep good company in those difficult days. Mother Teresa lived through an unusually long period of dryness and darkness in her own life of prayer, once writing, "When I try to raise my thoughts to Heaven—there is such convicting emptiness that those very thoughts return like sharp knives & hurt my very soul." In these dark times our longing for intimacy with God can be particularly acute and painfully unsatisfied.

When "the Word became flesh and lived among us" (John 1:14), when Jesus accepted the limitations of a human life in mortal flesh, he necessarily surrendered something of his sense of closeness, tasting for himself our profound sense of separation from the presence of God, our aloneness and spiritual homesickness. As the apostle Paul wrote, he

emptied himself . . .
being born in human likeness . . .
and became obedient to the point of death—
even death on a cross. (Philippians 2:7-8)

And nowhere more clearly than on the cross can we see Jesus' devastating pain as he is torn from his place of intimacy at the Father's side. His dying cry is the anguished lament of every soul alienated from God's presence, every heart that finds itself far from its divine home and isolated in this universe: "My God, my God, why have you forsaken me?" (Matthew 27:46). This is our cry, our longing, and our terror at its most severe.

The catastrophe of the cross had the potential to tear the universe apart. When stars collapse on themselves and their vast mass is pressed into an unimaginably tiny space, the resulting black hole becomes a place isolated from the rest of creation, from which even light itself cannot escape. Scientists speculate that these extraordinary phenomena may even cause breaches in space and time itself. But on the cross we find a shattering, not of the fabric of creation but of the inner life of the Creator. God himself, who sustains all life and matter in being from moment to moment, is torn in two. All history hung on a knife edge at Calvary; it could easily have begun the collapse of existence itself.

But instead, in the unexpected grace and providence of God, the cross became the supreme place of reconciliation, healing, and life, the event which made a renewed divine and human community possible. How this happened is a great mystery that resists all our attempts to reduce it to simple analogies and models. Scripture employs a variety of metaphors to explore (rather than explain) the consequences of the cross as they ripple across creation. Jesus is compared to both priest and sacrifice in the temple, repairing the relationship between God and his people (Hebrews 7:27). His death is the satisfaction of a legal debt that estranged two litigants in court (Colossians 2:14). He becomes an idealized representative of the human race whose life-giving obedience unravels the disobedience at the heart of our nature (Romans 5:18). He releases captives by paying the ransom for their lives in his own blood (Matthew 20:28). In relation to his crucifixion, Jesus is described as reconciler, example, and victor; his death heals relationships between divided peoples, between people and God, between God and the whole cosmos. It has repercussions that reach down to touch the lowliest individual and stretch out to encompass all creation.

But all these analogies point toward the same conclusion: that the death of Jesus is a pivotal moment for all creation. And his earliest followers recognized this profound significance wherever they told his story. The apostle Paul wrote in one of his letters: "When I came to you, brothers and sisters, I did not come proclaiming the mystery of God to you in lofty words or wisdom. For I decided to know nothing among you except Jesus Christ, and him crucified" (1 Corinthians 2:1-2). No wonder, then, that the Gospels, the first biographical narratives of Jesus' life and death, have sometimes been described as Passion narratives (that is, the narrative of his suffering and death) with somewhat lengthy introductions. This cross, this death, is in the end the great mystery of God that shapes all human history and the whole natural order. No wonder that the sixteenth-century Reformer Martin Luther emphatically insisted that *crux probat omnia*: "the cross tests everything."

INTO THE DARKNESS

It should come as no surprise, then, that for us too a life of ever-deepening intimacy with God will lead through surrender, pain, and darkness toward death. The earliest followers of Jesus accepted new members into their kingdom community by leading them through a ritual, symbolic death: the drowning that is baptism. Those who desired to participate in the community would be led into the flowing waters of a stream or river; water that flowed was believed to be, in some sense, "living water," and so could stand as a powerful sign of the new life being offered to the person being baptized. They would then be plunged into these waters of life "in the name of the Father and of the Son and of the Holy Spirit" (Matthew 28:19), that is, they were immersed into the loving community of the Trinity, the very heart of the kingdom community Jesus had announced.

But this immersion into a new life also involved death, an ending of the old life. Rebirth begins with a funeral, with the demise of the person we once were. The apostle Paul wrote very clearly about this to the church in Rome. "Do you not know," he asked them, "that all of us who have been baptized into Christ Jesus were baptized into his death? Therefore we have been buried with him by baptism into death, so that, just as Christ was raised from the dead by the glory of the Father, so we too might walk in newness of life" (Romans 6:3-4). In many parts of the Western world baptism has been tamed and integrated among the social niceties surrounding the birth of a baby, a sweet welcoming of our tender little ones into the world. It's hard to imagine that many parents, gathering around a font with their newborn wrapped in gorgeous silks and ribbons, have any conception that they are about to symbolically kill their child.

THE WAY OF SURRENDER

But it's equally hard for many of us to understand that a journey into ever greater intimacy with the Father will also lead us into darkness and death, into the surrender of all that matters to us, to our sense of self, and of our very lives.

Some of the most beautiful, haunting, and profound writing about this surrender of the soul and the darkness it leads us into came from the sixteenth-century Spanish writer Juan de Yepes y Álvarez, known to English speakers as John of the Cross. John was a member of the Carmelite monastic family and worked with his contemporary Teresa of Ávila to try to bring reform to the religious communities of his order. But these reforms, which sought to make life in the monasteries more rigorous and ascetic, were bitterly resisted, and in late 1577 John was captured by a group of fellow monks and spirited away to Toledo. Here he found himself imprisoned for many months under the most brutal conditions. He was placed in solitary confinement in a cell just ten feet long by six feet wide and kept in almost permanent darkness. His captors kept him on a meager diet of bread, fish, and water, and brought him out almost every week to be whipped in the presence of the rest of the community. All this was intended to compel John to renounce his involvement in the reforming movement. In fact, it served to drive him into a dark depression—but also to drive him more deeply into the heart of Christ.

During his imprisonment, John composed the "Spiritual Canticle," a poem describing in allegorical terms the journey of the soul into an ever more intimate relationship with God. (He held the entire poem in his memory until he was able to write it down after escaping captivity.) The poem speaks in moving terms of the road this journey takes through darkness, night, and the feeling of abandonment; it can be challenging and harrowing reading. The opening lines set the tone:

Where are you hiding,
Beloved, leaving me moaning?
You fled like the stag,
leaving me wounded;
I went out weeping, but you were gone.

But eventually the poet begins to sense that God is leading him to "solitary wooded valleys" and "strange islands," secluded places of darkness where he can become still enough to experience the "silent music" and "resonant solitude" of God's presence.

This later became a central theme in John's poetry, writing, and teaching. He spoke of the "dark night of the soul" in which the heart was slowly weaned from its dependence on exciting experiences of God, emotional and intellectual stimulation in prayer, and a relationship with God sweetened by special graces, gifts, and blessings. John began to seek to relinquish everything in his life other than the naked presence of God, unseen and unheard in the darkness, but present nonetheless. He imagined himself ascending the rugged mountain of the interior life to meet God, as Moses did, face to face; letting go of every encumbrance as he walked until he arrived at the summit with *nada, nada, nada*: nothing, nothing, nothing. John knew that the road to God could be painful.

Who would not want to rest their head on the Father's heart and listen to the divine whisper? To know him even as we are known? To enter into the friendships of the Trinity? The invitation is so attractive and compelling. But it is also costly and demanding. Our true home in God, for which we feel such longing, such *hiraeth*, is beautiful and wondrous and magnificent. But the voyage home can be agonizing, ghastly, and filled with sorrow. The invitation to rest at his side is open to all. But there is no head lying on his breast that is not scarred.

THE JOURNEY
INTO GOD

Across the centuries the followers of Jesus have described the journey into divine intimacy in a variety of ways, reflecting the diversity of people participating in the kingdom community and the uniqueness of each person's experience. But one description has proven particularly useful and durable, since it seems to capture the essence of the journey for so many. It became known as "the threefold way."

The eighteenth-century pastor and theologian Jonathan Edwards described the threefold way beautifully in his brief book *A Treatise Concerning Religious Affections*. "The nature of true grace and spiritual light," he wrote,

> opens to a person's view the infinite reason there is that he should be holy in a high degree. And the more grace he has, and the more this is opened to view, the greater sense he has of the infinite excellency and glory of the Divine Being, the infinite dignity of the person of Christ, and the boundless length and breadth and depth and height of the love of Christ to sinners. And as grace increases, the field opens more and more to a distant view, until the soul is swallowed up with the vastness of the object, and the person is astonished to think how much it becomes him to love this God, and this glorious Redeemer that has so loved man.

These three broad stages of the threefold way—from holiness of life, through growth in knowledge, to being "swallowed up" in Christ's love—can be described in gospel terms as *turning*, *knowing*, and *abiding*. (Historically, spiritual writers have more usually talked about *purgation*, *illumination*, and *union*. But while this technical language can be useful, particularly for scholars, for the rest of us it can be unfamiliar, confusing, and distracting.) We each experience these three stages differently, and for greatly varying periods of time in our lives. Although most people can discern a general movement over time from one to the next, there is a certain fluidity between them, and many will find themselves regressing to previous stages as often as they feel themselves to be moving forward. In short, the threefold way is by no means a perfect description of our growing intimacy with the Father. However, just as we can generalize about our experience of growing older (talking about such stages of life as childhood, adolescence, adulthood, old age) and still find these distinctions helpful despite all their imprecision, so this model of the three stages of our relationship with God has shown itself to be of tremendous value.

TOWARD GOD'S KINGDOM

The journey begins with *turning*, the orientation (or more accurately reorientation) of our life toward God and toward the loving community of God's kingdom. This brings us back to the drama of repentance, the transformation of outlook and life announced by Jesus as the precondition for participation in God's kingdom community: "The time is fulfilled, and the kingdom of God has come near; repent, and believe in the good news" (Mark 1:15). *Turning* is the movement of the heart that opens up the possibility of our transformation into greater Christlikeness, the reshaping of our lives from heart sickness to an inward reordering of love. It is the renewal of our inner and outer self by the Spirit of God that results from our immersion in God's life and presence.

Jesus constantly highlighted this reorientation toward God and other people as a sign that the reality of God's kingdom was breaking into a person's life. He warned the religious leaders of his day, who stood in violent opposition to his preaching of God's kingdom community, to learn from the outcasts and misfits who so gladly surrounded him: "Truly I tell you, the tax collectors and the prostitutes are going into the kingdom of God ahead of you" (Matthew 21:31). When the senior tax official Zacchaeus began publically reorienting his life around the call of God's kingdom, Jesus proclaimed to those around him, "Today salvation has come to this house" (Luke 19:9). During a debate with him in the temple courts in Jerusalem, a religious scholar made the extraordinary observation that "'to love [God] with all the heart, and with all the understanding, and with all the strength,' and 'to love one's neighbor as oneself,'—this is much more important than all whole burnt offerings and sacrifices." Jesus responded to this evidence of a reoriented heart by asserting: "You are not far from the kingdom of God" (Mark 12:33-34).

In John's Gospel we find Jesus employing an even more startling image. When the leader and Pharisee Nicodemus comes to discuss his teachings with him by night, Jesus warns him bluntly: "Very truly, I tell you, no one can see the kingdom of God without being born from above" (John 3:3). The image of rebirth is stark and uncompromising: it marks the ending of one life and the beginning of another, a life that can only emerge from death, the surrender of all we have been and all we have become. "Unless a grain of wheat falls into the earth and dies," Jesus tells his disciples later in the same Gospel, "it remains just a single grain; but if it dies, it bears much fruit" (John 12:24). This is the paradoxical dynamic of *metanoia*: "those who try to make their life secure will lose it, but those who lose their life will keep it" (Luke 17:33). No wonder, then, that after the dramatic turning around of his life on the Damascus road, the apostle Paul writes, "it is no longer I who live, but it is Christ who lives in me" (Galatians 2:20).

KNOWING GOD

As our hearts are reoriented toward God and his kingdom, the shape of our lives is slowly transformed by the Spirit, conforming more and more to the likeness of Jesus and exhibiting his essential characteristics: "love, joy, peace, patience, kindness, generosity, faithfulness, gentleness, and self-control" (Galatians 5:22-23). And along with this nurturing of the life of Christ within us we also find ourselves developing an ever-deepening understanding of the heart of God and the way that heart expresses itself in creation and in God's activity within our lives, our communities, and in history more broadly. "What human being knows what is truly human except the human spirit that is within?" asks Paul; in the same way "no one comprehends what is truly God's except the Spirit of God." But we have been given "the Spirit that is from God, so that we may understand the gifts bestowed on us by God," with the result that "we have the mind of Christ" (1 Corinthians 2:11-16). The growth involved in *turning*, then, leads inexorably to a richer *knowing* of God.

This knowledge is not an analytical, intellectual "knowing about" God, the ability to engage in the academic discipline of theology (although for some that discipline can enrich the journey into the spiritual *knowing* Paul describes); it is rather the experiential knowledge we have of food we have tasted, places we have visited, and people we have lived among. The philosopher Ludwig Wittgenstein wrestled with these two different kinds of knowledge in his *Philosophical Investigations*. "Describe the aroma of coffee," he wrote at one point. "Why can't it be done? Do we lack the words? And for what are words lacking? But how do we get the idea that such a description must after all be possible? Have you ever felt the lack of such a description? Have you tried to describe the aroma of coffee and not succeeded?" What we're seeking is not the knowledge of God we might glean from a book, but the experiential knowledge of Moses kneeling barefoot at the burning bush. We don't want to *explain* the coffee, we want to *drink* it.

One of the principal ways we can nurture this *knowing* of God within ourselves is through the prayerful reading of, and meditation on, Scripture. God's presence breathes through the pages of the Bible in a way that makes it unlike any other text, and generations of readers down the ages have been astonished at its ability not only to speak of God but to somehow make God present in the reader's experience. Followers of Christ, particularly within monastic communities, have found particular value in an approach to reading known as *lectio divina* or "sacred reading." *Lectio* provides a way for us to move beyond simply reading or even studying this remarkable text; it shows us how to open our hearts and lives both to the book itself and to the presence of the Spirit mediated to us through the act of reading.

The method of practicing *lectio divina* is easily described, although practitioners will be quick to point out that *method* is already an unhelpful word, implying a set of instructions to be slavishly followed. It might help instead to think of a landscape to be explored, the landscape of Scripture and of the human soul, and to think of the steps of this method as staging posts usually encountered as people journey through this landscape. With this in mind, *lectio* can be broken down into four stages: the initial act of reading itself, reflection and meditation on what has been read, being drawn into prayerful response to God, and a stilling of the mind and heart, which allows us to rest in silence in God's presence.

SACRED READING

It might help to use a concrete example to show what these steps look like. Imagine that you were beginning to read the book of the prophet Jeremiah. After a short introductory paragraph, the prophecies open with these words:

Now the word of the LORD came to me saying,
  "Before I formed you in the womb I knew you,

and before you were born I consecrated you;

I appointed you a prophet to the nations."

Then I said, "Ah, Lord GOD! Truly I do not know how to speak,

for I am only a boy." (Jeremiah 1:4-6)

Our first step, then, is simply to *read* these words, slowly, attentively, carefully. Many people find it helpful to read aloud since it often aids concentration and helps us notice unusual phrases or ideas more clearly.

After reading the words we begin to *reflect* on them. Since we're seeking an experience of God, not simply information about the ancient text of the Bible, this reflection shouldn't be confused with academic study: we're not primarily concerned here with questions of translation from the original languages, insights from archaeological investigations, or efforts to reconcile the passage in hand with a wider systematic interpretation of the book, the prophets as a body, or the whole Bible (although these are all good and helpful reading strategies in other contexts). Our primary question is how this text can bring us to a fuller experiential knowledge of God.

In our reflection we allow the text to gather up from our memory any and every other resonance it forms with the rest of Scripture. In "the word of the Lord came to me" we may hear echoes of the creation story, where God brings all things into being by his word (Genesis 1:1–2:4); we might think of the word coming to the boy Samuel as he slept in the temple (1 Samuel 3:1-10); perhaps we think of God's Word personified in Jesus coming to the apostle John during his exile in Patmos (Revelation 1:9-20); and even of John's magnificent hymn of praise to the Word made flesh (John 1:1-18). In all this we notice the primacy of God's action, God taking the initiative to create, to call, to speak, to rebuke, and to love. That sense of God's initiative is reinforced as we continue to read about Jeremiah being known and consecrated before his birth—and again we may be reminded of other biblical passages: the promise of Isaac's birth to Abraham and Sarah (Genesis 18:1-15); the psalmist's wonder that "you knit me together in my mother's womb" (Psalm 139:13); or the promise of Christ given to the young Nazarene girl Mary (Luke 1:26-38). But we are also attentive to Jeremiah's reluctance and fear, so similar to that of Moses at the burning bush (Exodus 4:13), Jonah when asked to preach to his enemies in Nineveh (Jonah 1:1-3), or Peter when first called by Jesus (Luke 5:8).

Attentive to these biblical dynamics of God's primacy of action, of the power of his word spoken into people's lives, of his purpose bringing us into being, and of our own reluctance and fear when faced with this reality, we allow the passage to lead us into prayerful *response*. Asking the Spirit to speak God's Word into our spirit, we listen for his call to us, the call he has been preparing us for from before the day of our birth. And we open up our hearts to him, sharing the fears, uncertainties, and reluctance that hinder us from responding fully to that call, pleading for his transforming grace to bring us healing and courage. Our prayer might well—in time, *should*—spill out beyond ourselves to draw in our families, neighborhoods, communities, and nations: how can we learn together to listen to God's voice and respond with freedom and joy?

In time we find these words of prayer drawing to an end; the final stage of *lectio* is an encouragement not to rush on to the next activity of the day but rather to dwell in the presence of God in stillness. We find ourselves at *rest* in silence. And this brings us not only to the final stage of *lectio divina* but also to the third part of the threefold way: *abiding*. "Abide in me as I abide in you," Jesus invited his disciples (John 15:4), having already promised them that "those who love me will keep my word, and my Father will love them, and we will come to them and make our home with them" (John 14:23).

And so we find ourselves beginning to enjoy the intimacy of *hiraeth* fulfilled: having found our way into the Father's presence we can lean back against his breast, listening for the divine whisper if he chooses to speak, but content simply to be with him. And while the journey to this place of rest and receptivity can be hard, and we can find ourselves stripped down and painstakingly remade along the way, we arrive grateful. After all, we are finally where we belong: close to the Father's heart. Our long and challenging road has, in the end, brought us home.

OVER TO YOU

Scripture and Reflection

W E BEGAN THIS SECTION BY IDENTIFYING the deep yearning of the human heart to dwell in God's presence. We saw that Jesus repeatedly invited people into this experience, a life lived "close to the Father's heart," and that he spoke of this intimate relationship in terms of both eternal life and life in the kingdom. But we also discovered that this intimacy comes at great cost, as we die to our old life in order to be born anew (an experience mirrored in the practice of baptism). We looked at the ancient tradition of a spiritual journey into God marked by *turning*, *knowing*, and *abiding*. Finally, we considered how prayerful reading of Scripture can lead us through this journey into an experience of intimacy.

The following readings and questions may help you reflect further on this in your own life. The seven readings and reflections could be used on a daily basis over the next week. Or you may prefer simply to tackle the questions and ideas that stand out to you right now.

• *Song of Songs 7:10–8:4*

Have you ever experienced a yearning of the heart for God, as a lover longs for their beloved? How comfortable are you with thinking of your life with God in those terms?

- *John 14:1-7*

   How do you feel about Jesus' invitation to dwell in intimacy with the Father? Does it attract you, or do you find it difficult?

- *John 15:1-11*

   What does it mean to you to abide in Christ? What helps you most in doing that?

- *Matthew 27:45-54*

   How would you describe Jesus' experience on the cross? How would you describe its impact on your own life?

- *Romans 6:1-11*

   In what ways have you experienced death to your old self, and burial, and new life in Jesus?

- *Isaiah 35:8-10*

   How would you describe the stages of your own spiritual journey so far? What do you think might be coming next?

- *Revelation 10:8-10*

   How do you "eat" the Scriptures—take them into your inner self and allow them to become part of you? What difference has that made in your life?

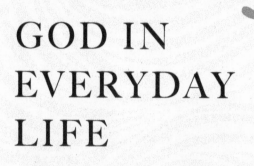

GOD IN EVERYDAY LIFE

We nurture intimacy with God
in the sacraments of everyday life.

GOD IN ALL THINGS

LEARNING TO SEE

LEARNING ATTENTIVENESS

OVER TO YOU

GOD IN
ALL THINGS

THIS MORNING I WALKED ALONG a lane near my home and picked up a beech leaf from the road; I have it on the desk in front of me as I write. Mostly pale green, its surface is mottled with some slightly darker patches; its edges are rumpled (largely from being carried in my pocket); its tip is missing, torn off. It is unmistakably a beech leaf, instantly recognizable by its toothed edges and classic, childlike leaf shape; it is indistinguishable at first glance from any other beech leaf. Yet at the same time it is utterly unique. The marbled colors, the patterning of veins under its surface, its particular shape and contours, its history—all these set it apart from everything else in existence. Even given the unimaginably long history and vastness of the universe, it is an occurrence that will never be seen again until the end of the ages.

The nineteenth-century English poet Gerard Manley Hopkins rejoiced in this singularity to be found everywhere in creation, in the profound individuality of everything that is. "Glory be to God for dappled things," he wrote; for

All things counter, original, spare, strange;
Whatever is fickle, freckled (who knows how?)
With swift, slow; sweet, sour; adazzle, dim;
He fathers-forth whose beauty is past change:
Praise him.

But Hopkins was not simply another Romantic poet celebrating the prettiness of the natural world. During his training as a Jesuit priest Hopkins had been captivated by the writings of the great medieval philosopher and theologian John Duns Scotus, and particularly by Scotus's reflections on uniqueness and individuality. The detailed and obscure writings of this thirteenth-century thinker caused Hopkins to see the world in an entirely new light.

A GLORIOUS INDIVIDUALITY

Before Scotus, philosophers had commonly spoken of the essence of an individual object as its *quiddity*; the Latin word *quid* means "what," and *quiddity* is the "whatness" of an object—that which makes the object what it is. Aristotle, for example, has the *quiddity* of a human being, while his pet, Skylos, has the *quiddity* of a dog. The leaf on my desk has saw-toothed edges and a bright green hue, elements of the *quiddity* of a beech leaf.

But Scotus wanted to take his reflections about essence deeper. Aristotle has the *quiddity* of a human being, but so does Plato or Socrates or John Duns Scotus. What, then, is the difference between them? Are they all essentially identical, all simply examples of the one idea of a human person? Or is there some way we can distinguish one from the next?

To answer that question, Scotus developed the idea of *haecceity*. The Latin word *haec* means "this," and while *quiddity* describes the "whatness" of an object, *haecceity* speaks of its "thisness." Arms, legs, and a reasoning mind help define the *quiddity* of a human being, whether Aristotle or Plato. But the curled hair, snub nose, mischievous sense of humor, and fondness for playful conversation mark out *this* human being among all others: it can only be Plato, not Aristotle or Scotus or anyone else. Or with my leaf, its sawed edge and tapered shape have the *quiddity* of a beech leaf, but the mottled surface and torn tip set *this* leaf apart from all others: they are part of its *haecceity*.

Hopkins coined his own term, *inscape*, to describe this quality found in all existing things. For Hopkins an object's inscape was its inner landscape, the vast interior uniqueness that would unfold itself to any patient observer willing to look for it. The experience of this inscape revealing itself to a person he called *instress*, and in his poetry he tried to capture his own sense of *instress* in words that might evoke a parallel response in his readers. He believed that inscape was present in everything, large and small, but it took time to learn to see it well. "I saw the inscape … freshly, as if my eyes were still growing," he wrote following a walk on the Bowland Fells with a friend, "though with a companion the eye and ear are for the most part shut and instress cannot come." But on another occasion he was more successful in remaining open to the experience. "What you look at hard seems to look back at you," he recollected afterwards. "Unless you refresh the mind from time to time you cannot always remember or believe how deep the inscape in things is." And although the inscape can be dulled or blunted by the human abuse of nature, can "wear man's smudge and share man's smell," nevertheless

The world is charged with the grandeur of God.
It will flame out, like shining from shook foil;
It gathers to a greatness, like the ooze of oil
Crushed …
… nature is never spent;
There lives the dearest freshness deep down things.

The beauty, graciousness, mercy, and exuberant joy of the Creator remains written into the very fabric of his creation and can be seen by any who choose to look. This world, for those who know how to see, is simply the kingdom made visible.

BIRDS OF THE AIR

It's not only from medieval philosophers and Victorian poets that we learn this: the revelation of God's nature and purposes through the world around us (both the world of nature and other human beings) was a central theme of Jesus' teaching in the Gospels.

"Look at the birds of the air," was the counsel Jesus offered to those who wanted to understand the merciful providence of God. "They neither sow nor reap nor gather into barns, and yet your heavenly Father feeds them. Are you not of more value than they?" (Matthew 6:26). On another occasion the birds once again revealed God's overseeing care: "Are not two sparrows sold for a penny? Yet not one of them will fall to the ground apart from your Father. And even the hairs of your head are all counted. So do not be afraid; you are of more value than many sparrows" (Matthew 10:29-31).

Along with the birds, the fields they flew over also spoke of God's nature. "Consider the lilies of the field, how they grow; they neither toil nor spin, yet I tell you, even Solomon in all his glory was not clothed like one of these" (Matthew 6:28-29). Considering the growth of plants in the fields was a favorite theme for Jesus; he returned to it repeatedly. In one beautiful illustration, Jesus highlighted the profound sense of mystery experienced by those who watched the fruits of the earth emerge from the ground, shooting up from tiny seed into full-grown plant:

> The kingdom of God is as if someone would scatter seed on the ground, and would sleep and rise night and day, and the seed would sprout and grow, he does not know how. The earth produces of itself, first the stalk, then the head, then the full grain in the head. (Mark 4:26-28)

Jesus saw this as the perfect mirror of the emergence of God's gift of the kingdom; it appears in the midst of us, unsought and undeserved, growing from near invisibility to become the driving force of history; it is "like a mustard seed that someone took and sowed in his field; it is the smallest of all the seeds, but when it has grown it is the greatest of shrubs and becomes a tree, so that the birds of the air come and make nests in its branches" (Matthew 13:31-32).

The kingdom is like good seed growing among wheat, showing itself in the midst of human brokenness (Matthew 13:24-30). Those who announce the coming of the kingdom are sowers of seed seeking good and responsive soil (Luke 8:4-8). A barren fig tree is given more time to bear fruit, just as God's mercy is patient with us in our fruitless pursuit of self-interest (Luke 13:6-9), whereas a budding fig tree can act as a sign of the immanence of the kingdom (Luke 21:29-33).

Everywhere Jesus looked he saw the hidden spiritual world opening itself up to view through the ordinary, the mundane, the everyday: wine at a wedding (John 2:1-11), salt in the kitchen (Matthew 5:13), water drawn from a well (John 4:13-14), leaven kneaded into bread dough (Luke 13:20-21). It was apparent in the dealings of merchants (Matthew 13:45-46) and the catch hauled in by fishermen (Matthew 13:47-50), in the care of the shepherd (Luke 15:3-7) or a woman cleaning her house (Luke 15:8-10). Above all it was revealed in people: in children (Matthew 19:14), in those set free from evil (Matthew 12:28), even in the lives of the despised tax collectors and prostitutes who were discovering kingdom mercy for themselves (Matthew 21:31).

The kingdom, it turns out, can be seen everywhere. The question is, do we have the eyes to see it?

LEARNING
TO SEE

KNOWING THAT THE KINGDOM *can* be seen and actually *seeing* it are two very different things. It takes practice to develop that kind of spiritual discernment, and the truth is that most of us struggle to see the simplest things right under our noses. A few years ago I decided to learn what it might mean to see a tree. I discovered that it's considerably more difficult than it sounds.

I'd been reading the classic seventeenth-century book about Brother Lawrence of the Resurrection, *The Practice of the Presence of God*. The author, a French priest named Joseph de Beaufort, describes a series of conversations he had with Lawrence about prayer and the constant awareness of God's presence. And he opens his description of the conversations with a brief summary of Lawrence's life, including an anecdote about an early spiritual experience: "One day in winter while he was looking at a tree stripped of its leaves, and he realized that in a little while its leaves would reappear, followed by its flowers and fruit, he received a profound insight into God's providence that has never been erased from his soul."

It's a fascinating and intriguing story. What could this young man, standing in front of a bare tree in the cold of winter, possibly have experienced that might still be affecting his life four decades later? I was eager to know. So one winter's morning I went out into the front yard of the Colorado house where I was living at the time and positioned myself uncertainly beside the young cherry tree in the middle of the lawn. I prayed briefly, asking God to let me share a little in whatever it was that had unfolded in Lawrence's heart. And I began to look.

The minutes ticked away and nothing happened. No revelation, no epiphany. I stood, shivering a little from the cold, and watched. After about twenty minutes I went back inside, none the wiser.

The next day I stood out on the lawn for another twenty minutes and waited. And the next day, and the next. Days turned to weeks. A kind of grim determination had taken hold of my soul: I was sure there was something important to be learned here, and I was determined not to miss it. Day after day I patiently stood and contemplated that tree, feeling cold and foolish.

It was months later that I finally saw a tree, and when it happened it wasn't even *my* tree. I was sitting in church one morning the following spring, my thoughts wandering, and I noticed one of the trees outside was beginning to bud. I began to try to count the buds (it was a really engaging sermon) and quickly lost track; there were so many. Something about this snagged at my spirit, so after the service I went outside and stood under the tree, trying to count the buds again. Such an abundance of emerging life! It suddenly felt as though this tree were bursting out of the ground and stretching its limbs into heaven in joyful exuberance; I wondered whether, if I were to reach out and touch the trunk, I might feel the sap throbbing under the bark. This tree was so alive—*this* tree, *this* tree! And suddenly I saw it, what Gerard Manley Hopkins would have called the "inscape" of the tree, the living organism in all its uniqueness and wonder.

I hurried home and stood under my tree. And saw it, really saw it; so different from the tree at church, so individual and marvelous, so vibrant and beautiful.

CAN YOU SEE?

Really seeing is difficult and takes time. If seeing a tree, which oblig-
ingly stays still and silent, offering itself to be seen, is such a challenge,
how hard might it be to see a storm, a river, a sunset—let alone another
person, made in the mysterious and incomprehensible image of God?

The Gospel of Luke tells a story about Jesus visiting the home of
a prominent religious leader, Simon the Pharisee (Luke 7:36-50).
During dinner a local woman, clearly known to all at the table for her
immoral reputation, slipped into the room uninvited and knelt at
Jesus' feet. (Jesus, like the other guests at the meal, would have been
reclining on the floor around a low table as we learned in an earlier
chapter, so her actions would have brought her uncomfortably close
not only to him but also to the other diners.) To Simon's horror this
disreputable woman began openly weeping, and as her tears fell onto
Jesus' feet she bent down to wipe them with her hair, which she was
obviously wearing loose rather than properly tied up: the usual habit
of prostitutes. Then, making matters even worse, she began kissing
his feet and, taking an alabaster jar of scent, which surely was one of
her alluring "tools of the trade," she began pouring the expensive
perfume over them.

Simon was scandalized and began to project his discomfort onto
Jesus. "If this man were a prophet," he thought to himself, "he would
have known who and what kind of woman this is who is touching
him—that she is a sinner" (Luke 7:39). In response to this unspoken
thought of Simon's, Jesus told a story. A lender was owed money by
two people; one owed around two months' wages and the other almost
two years' worth. But the lender forgave them both. So which of these,
Jesus asked, loved the lender more? Simon made the obvious choice:
the one who owed more. Then, calling everyone's attention to the
woman, Jesus contrasted her loving behavior with Simon's rather
lackadaisical neglect of his guest: where Simon had omitted the
customs of greeting with a kiss and offering scented water to clean up

after the journey to his house (these were important elements of Middle Eastern hospitality), the woman had showered an abundance of love on Jesus through her tears and perfume. Turning to the woman, Jesus told her, "Your sins are forgiven"—to her evident joy, but to the consternation of the other guests.

What made Jesus so attentive to the way God was present and at work in this woman's life? Above all else it was her *love*. "Her sins, which were many, have been forgiven," Jesus tells Simon, "hence she has shown great love. But the one to whom little is forgiven, loves little" (Luke 7:47). Later in the New Testament the apostle Paul identifies a variety of related "fruit of the Spirit" which, in addition to being the evidence and outworking of the Spirit's transformation of the soul, are often indicators of the Spirit's activity in a person's life: "love, joy, peace, patience, kindness, generosity, faithfulness, gentleness, and self-control" (Galatians 5:22-23). Of course, there's no simple identification between these attributes and the divine work of the Spirit: people are sometimes patient or kind all by themselves. But a person being touched or shaped by God's Spirit is increasingly likely to display these qualities, so if we're wise we'll pay attention whenever we come across them. And, as Paul writes elsewhere, "the greatest of these is love" (1 Corinthians 13:13), so whenever we encounter deep, sacrificial, and self-giving love, it's worth being open to the possibility that God's Spirit is powerfully present and active.

In the midst of his mealtime conversation with Simon, Jesus asks a question of great importance, a seemingly simple question around which the whole conversation then turns. Having compared the loves of the two forgiven creditors, and before he compares the behavior of Simon and the visitor at dinner, we're told that "turning toward the woman, he said to Simon, 'Do you see this woman?'" (Luke 7:44).

There, in a nutshell, was Simon's problem. He simply didn't see the woman. When she walked into his house he had seen her reputation and history. He had seen her immorality and dirtiness. He had seen, perhaps, the revulsion of some of his guests, and seen the echo of that in his own heart. He had seen an issue, a problem, a scandal. And being unable to see the woman he was entirely incapable of seeing how the Spirit might be at work in the woman's life. He was so caught up in his own inner turmoil he was unable to recognize another human being; in his comparative lovelessness, he could not see how God might be present and at work in the midst of his dinner party.

But where Simon saw a scandal, Jesus saw a beauty and a marvel. He saw this woman as she was: a creation of God, bearing God's image and likeness, radiating God's beauty even in her brokenness. He saw not only what she had made of herself but also what God had made her, and what God longed for her to be. He saw her *love*, together with her sorrow, and the touch of grace and mercy on her life. And seeing this, he saw what underlay it: the presence of God in her life.

THE GIFT OF PEOPLE

I'll be honest: I struggle with this myself. Some people seem to be naturally people focused, always very aware of other folks around them, their emotions and reactions, their stories and connections with one another. Others are more task focused, centered on the work and projects at hand and less aware of the people in their environment who are contributing to (or interfering with) those tasks. For my part, I have a tendency to be ideas focused, less aware of either the people around me or the work at hand, and mostly fascinated with theories, concepts, blue-sky thinking, and exploring possibilities. In a creative brainstorming session I can really hum, but I've had to work hard to develop the skills to be an organized work colleague and an attentive pastor.

But I think that for most of us it takes deliberate, intentional effort and a lot of practice to really see people. Being naturally people focused, more drawn to people's company than their work or ideas, is one thing; truly centering your attention on another person is something else again. It requires us to cultivate a kind of inner hospitality, which can be quite costly.

Hospitality always involves creating space for other people. When we prepare a guest room for a visitor, we set aside space within our own home and make it available to the guest when they arrive. For the duration of their stay, that room becomes our gift to them: most people, having given the gift, would feel they were being rude if they took it back again by intruding on that space. So we tend not to go into the guest's room without their permission—even though it's really our room, in our own home! In our act of hospitality, we have chosen to give something of ourselves away to another person.

Truly seeing people springs from a hospitality of the soul. We have to create space within our very selves where the other person can dwell and flourish. So, for a time at least, we have to set aside our own agendas, our timetables, our to-do lists and preoccupations. Genuine listening and attention means becoming open to the other person's story without concern for our own reaction and response; this can be extremely challenging. Like me, you can probably remember countless conversations when you realize you've been so busy thinking about what you're going to say next, you've stopped hearing what the other person is saying. In those moments, we've withdrawn our heart's hospitality.

Perhaps we can learn here from Jesus. It's interesting that in the Gospels we find phrases such as "Jesus said to him," "Jesus replied," "Answering them, Jesus said," or "Jesus cried out." But we never hear "Jesus interrupted him" or "Changing the subject, Jesus said" or "Jesus asked him to repeat what he'd just said." It's also noticeable that Jesus often asked people questions—genuine questions, not just rhetorical flourishes to steer the conversation—and always gave space for people to respond. On some occasions, he happily gave his respondents the last word, simply affirming their answers: "You are not far from the kingdom of God" (Mark 12:34) or "You have given the right answer" (Luke 10:28).

"Do you see this woman?" Jesus asked Simon. It turns out to be much harder than it sounds; the work, maybe, of a lifetime. And if seeing another person is this challenging, how might we begin to open ourselves to the experience of the presence of God?

LEARNING
ATTENTIVENESS

Brother Lawrence spoke about the "practice of the presence of God" as an intentional activity, a habit we can learn and cultivate, rather than an inherent inclination or personality trait. It's tempting to talk as though some people in this world are more "spiritual" and "reflective" while others are "practical" and "down to earth"; the business of tuning in to God's presence then becomes the preserve of the religious and introspective types. But it's simply not true: in my experience it's no easier or harder for any given person to develop attentiveness to the presence of God. Those who are most aware of God's presence in their day-to-day lives are usually those who've troubled to train themselves in being aware.

One helpful way of learning to recognize that presence is an ancient practice known as *examen*. Drawn from the old Latin word for the indicator needle on a pair of weighing scales, examen invites us to weigh the events of each day in order to discern how God might have been at work in them, and how well or badly we've responded to that. Since it is an exercise most easily done after the event, it is one step removed from the moment right in front of us, but it does help to hone our spiritual attention.

In its simplest form examen simply involves taking a few minutes each evening to review the events of the day and ask two complementary questions. In its classic form the two questions were: Where did I experience consolation? and Where did I experience desolation?

Consolation is one of the more obvious signs of God's presence and work in our lives. Paul wrote in the New Testament about "the God of all consolation" and the "consolation [that] is abundant through Christ" (2 Corinthians 1:3-5), and we do often discover that God gives encouragement in our brightest moments and strength on our darkest days. By contrast, desolation, the sense of spiritual emptiness, is often a powerful indicator of God's absence. Recognizing whether our consolation genuinely stems from the Spirit, or when God is present to us even in the midst of the deepest desolation, requires a great deal of experience in the spiritual life together with a measure of wisdom and discernment. But in general these two questions can provide a helpful lens through which to review our day-to-day lives, to discover where God has been most active and where least present—and to ask why.

There are other ways of framing these questions. Some prefer to ask, What today has been life-giving? And what has been life-denying? Or, more directly, some will ask, Where has God been present? And where has God been absent? (Although, peculiarly, many people find it harder to recognize God's presence and activity when looking for it so straightforwardly; often the indirect glance can be more fruitful.)

One pair of questions that might be particularly helpful in our context would be: Where today have I experienced loving community? and Where have I experienced the loss of love and community? One by one we allow the events of the day to rise up in our memory and weigh them against these two questions. Breakfast with the family. Riding to work on the train or bus. Walking in the park with a friend. An argument with a colleague at work. Handling a difficult phone call. Sharing a meal with friends. Without criticism or judgment, either of ourselves or of others, we simply ask where love and community were evident and where they were lacking. And as we do this we learn to recognize the subtle signs of the Spirit's work in our everyday lives, in the ordinary events of each mundane day. Perhaps we had a challenging conversation with a neighbor but were surprised to find it ended with some degree of agreement, a more amicable resolution than we expected. Can we see the gentle work of God in this? On the other hand, in the angry complaint we made to the woman working in the coffee shop can we sense the breakdown in community we caused as we ceased to allow the Spirit to speak kindness through us?

To engage in this examen once can be an intriguing and interesting experience of an ancient spiritual discipline. Over a few days it becomes a little more illuminating. But it is most powerful when practiced over many months or years, even if only for a few minutes each day. We slowly accrue an accumulation of wisdom about the day-to-day activity of God in our ordinary lives, noticing patterns of presence and absence, and understanding more fully our response to God's actions.

As we practice this examen, continually reviewing our days seeking to recognize God's presence, we also become far more attuned to noticing that presence *in the moment*, as events are unfolding. The presence of God we have taught ourselves to look for retrospectively becomes more immediately apparent. If we have also taught ourselves to become increasingly attentive to the present moment in which God is present and active, we may discover that the mysterious breathing of the Spirit through our life and the lives of others around us is far more visible than we ever suspected. Because we are looking, we begin to see.

WAYS TO REMEMBER

Our next problem, of course, is that we forget. We see once, but then our attention drifts away; it is caught up in the anxieties of the day, it is distracted by busyness and bustle. We need constant reminders.

The early generations of Jesus-followers developed a collection of reminders of the presence of God in our midst; they called them "sacraments." Over the centuries that word became contentious and divisive, tied up in wranglings and arguments about authority in the community and the interpretation of Scripture—debates which lie far beyond the scope of this book. But in its essence, the idea remains extremely useful.

The basic definition of a sacrament is simple: "an outward and visible sign of an inward and spiritual grace." It's easy to illustrate. Imagine a group of disciples of Jesus gathered in someone's home in first-century Rome. Following the lead of the Gospel stories, during their worship they take bread, bless it, break it, and share it with one another. Then they bless a cup of wine and share that too, a deliberate repetition of the actions of Jesus at the Last Supper in obedience to his straightforward command: "Do this in remembrance of me" (Luke 22:19).

This would be a great example of a sacrament. The "outward and visible" sign would be the broken bread and shared cup. The "inward and spiritual grace" would be the presence of Jesus in some way made more imminent and real among the disciples as they share the meal together. (People have furiously debated exactly *how* Jesus might become more present through this sacrament, and have used those arguments to break the community of Jesus-followers over and over again in one of the greatest ironies of the whole history of the Jesus movement. It's tragic and senseless, but fortunately we don't need to resolve it here in order to understand the basic concept of a sacrament.)

The idea of a sacrament captures something essential to the teaching of Jesus in the Gospels: the kingdom is revealed in the ordinariness of everyday life. God makes himself known in the simplicity of bread and wine (or in water at baptism or oil used for anointing). The kingdom, which can be seen passively in the growing seed and rising dough, in the birds of the air and children in the streets, in the work of a farmer, merchant, accountant, or mother, can also be brought to the surface actively in our meals, our washing, our service of one another. Sacraments are powerful signs of grace in action.

It's odd, then, that historically the community of Christ's disciples have worked extremely hard to restrict the sacraments. We've tried to confine them to the smallest possible number: perhaps just seven, or only two, or maybe none at all. And we've insisted they be celebrated by the minimum number of people: just the leaders, the ordained, the anointed, the set aside. Perhaps the problem is that we should have been doing precisely the opposite: as many outward and visible signs as we could possibly imagine, celebrated by as many followers of Jesus as we could muster.

CREATIVE REMINDERS

I wonder whether what we really need are more *mezuzot*, a beautiful Jewish tradition of remembrance. In the biblical book of Deuteronomy Moses encourages the Israelites to be creative about keeping the call to love God at the forefront of their consciousness:

> Hear, O Israel: The LORD is our God, the LORD alone. You shall love the LORD your God with all your heart, and with all your soul, and with all your might. Keep these words that I am commanding you today in your heart. Recite them to your children and talk about them when you are at home and when you are away, when you lie down and when you rise. Bind them as a sign on your hand, fix them as an emblem on your forehead, and write them on the doorposts of your house and on your gates. (Deuteronomy 6:4-9)

Inspired by these words, Jews have developed the practice of affixing a *mezuzah* on the doorframes of their homes. A *mezuzah* consists of a tiny rolled up scroll with Hebrew texts (including the passage from Deuteronomy 6) lovingly and prayerfully written on it by a trained scribe. The scroll is placed into a decorated case and attached to the doorpost. It is always placed at around shoulder height where is cannot fail to be noticed; many families attach the *mezuzah* at an angle in obedience to an old rabbinical custom that simply draws attention to it even more. Some people are in the habit of always touching (or even kissing) a *mezuzah* when they enter a home or room, perhaps uttering a brief prayer at the same time.

The purpose of placing *mezuzot* around the home is to act as a constant reminder of God's love, that he will "keep your going out and your coming in from this time on and forevermore" (Psalm 121:8), and of God's call to us to offer love in return. Interestingly, recent research has confirmed our human need for such tangible reminders. In a 2011 paper tellingly titled "Walking Through Doorways Causes Forgetting," the psychologist Gabriel Radvansky described the phenomenon of "resetting" mental focus that people seem to experience when moving from one room to another. After entering a room it's common for us to forget what we were doing in the previous room and why we came into the new one. How often do we find ourselves asking, *Now why did I come in here?* A *mezuzah* graciously addresses this very human foible, acting as a reminder to us that God is present as we cross every threshold, and that above all we are invited into this new home or new room in order to love. It's a kingdom sacrament, a visible sign of the invisible grace of God among us.

Of course, a *mezuzah* is intentionally sacramental: that is, it speaks to us of God because we choose to make that association. We deliberately create the spiritual significance of this object. But exposure to what is *intentionally* sacramental sensitizes us to all that is *inherently* sacramental. That is, when we break bread together we consciously invoke the memory of Jesus, but it also reminds us of the holiness of every meal we share; it alerts our spiritual senses. Every time we touch a *mezuzah* we find that these intentionally placed symbols strengthen in us the sense of God's constant presence, even when later we are in homes and places that have nothing fixed to their doorways. We are, by nature, forgetful and easily distracted. We need reminders, sacraments, *mezuzot*.

That's why it makes sense to fill our lives with sacraments, with outward and visible signs of God's inward and spiritual grace at work among us. By all means let us break bread together, anoint one another with oil, immerse each other in water, and exchange rings while we vow our lives to one another. Let's festoon our homes with *mezuzot* and icons, with candles and carvings, with biblical texts carved on our mantelpieces. Let's carry prayer beads in a pocket or wear a cross on our lapel or paint a small dot on the face of a watch to remind us to pray every time we check the time. Let's embrace the arts, celebrate the material, love the physicality of this world through which God makes himself known to us, learning with the poet William Blake:

> To see a World in a Grain of Sand,
> And a Heaven in a Wild Flower,
> Hold Infinity in the palm of your hand,
> And Eternity in an hour.

After all, can we really ever have too much "inward and spiritual grace"?

OVER TO YOU

Scripture and Reflection

I n these chapters we looked at the way the entire cosmos, an expansive gift of God, speaks to us of his nature, his character, and his kingdom. We explored Duns Scotus's idea of *haecceity*, the quality unique to each existing thing, which was so celebrated in Hopkins's poetry. We considered the ways in which this vibrant vision of God revealed through creation was expressed throughout the teaching of Jesus. We considered the difficulty of being attentive to the everyday world around us and the value of learning to see the simplest things. We considered how the ancient practice of examen might help us to develop our discernment of God's presence. We reflected on the value of sacraments in our own lives and communities, and the potential of *mezuzot* to help us remember to look for God's self-revelation through all that he has made.

This set of questions and readings may help you to consider these ideas and take your own thinking further. As before, you may wish to pick out a handful of especially helpful reflections or simply take each day's reading and questions as a daily exercise over the next week.

- *Psalm 8*

    When you consider the works of God's hands, does it help you become more aware of his presence? When is the beauty of creation helpful, and when a distraction?

- *Romans 1:16-23*

  How clearly do you think creation speaks to us of God's character? How difficult is it for us, with our disordered hearts and minds, to see clearly how creation speaks?

- *Hebrews 4:1-7*

  Do you find it easy or difficult to live in "today," in the present moment? What helps you, and what prevents you?

- *Psalm 139:7-12*

  How easy is it for you to be aware of God's presence in your day-to-day life? What helps or hinders your attentiveness?

- *1 Corinthians 11:23-26*

  How has sharing the broken bread with others nourished your relationship with God and with them? If this is not part of your community's tradition, in what ways do you physically express your spiritual life together?

- *Acts 19:11-20*

  Have you ever experienced unusual and surprising "sacraments" (like Paul's handkerchiefs and aprons)? When are such things useful, and when do they become misleading or a hindrance?

- *Deuteronomy 6:1-9*

  What are the *mezuzot* in your life, the things that remind you of God's presence in your life? What could become a *mezuzah* for you?

CREATING COMMUNITY

*We share life together with love,
grace, mercy, and reconciliation.*

LOVE WITHOUT BORDERS

THE GREAT COMMISSION

LEARNING LOVE IN GENTLENESS

OVER TO YOU

LOVE WITHOUT
BORDERS

I T WAS A SUMMER EVENING in early fourth-century Egypt and a young man languished miserably in the belly of a boat sailing along the Nile. Just a few hours earlier Pachomius had been sitting under a canopy in the marketplace drinking a cool barley beer with half a dozen friends while the heat of midday passed. Amoun had looked over his shoulder and whispered, "Trouble coming, my friend." And turning, Pachomius had seen the knot of Roman auxiliaries approaching. He remembered the rough, snide orders of one of the soldiers barked in his direction, a scuffle, and then the small group of youths being marched through the street with Shenoute nursing a badly bruised arm and Amoun bleeding from a cut above his eye. And just like that, Pachomius began a career in the Roman Army, the latest involuntary conscript for Caesar.

The boat pulled up to a jetty in Thebes, and Pachomius and his friends were roughly hauled ashore. The auxiliaries marched them to a small military enclosure where they found themselves locked for the night in a makeshift prison. As evening drew in, a gloomy silence settled over the group; even Shenoute's usual good humor had deserted him.

Then from the darkness outside came footsteps, voices, the sound of conversation: people chatting amiably with the guards. "You may," replied one of the soldiers to an unheard question. "Thank you," came the gentle reply, "and here's something for you too, my friend." The soldier grunted.

Then the door opened and five people came in: two older men, faces burned and wrinkled from years spent laboring in the burning sun, and three young boys carrying packs and bundles. One of the old men stretched out his hands in greeting. "My friends! You've had a hard day. Come sit with me; I have water and food. And this young man, Pishoy, has a bundle of clean clothes; something here may fit you. Come, wash and eat." He turned to Amoun. "Perhaps you'll let me clean that wound?"

Pachomius stepped toward him, wary. "Old man, we don't have any money for you. The soldiers took everything from us. We're poor customers for your goods, I'm afraid."

The old man grinned. "Well then, it's your lucky day, my friend! No money is exactly how much I'm looking for. These are gifts. The food, drink, clothes—we don't want anything for them. Just come and join us. You're tired and hungry. Eat. You'll feel better."

Pachomius paused—but then hunger overcame his caution. He took a half loaf of bread from the hands of one of the boys and greedily bit into it. It was good, still warm! He motioned the others to join him, and the boys unpacked an unprepossessing but (to Pachomius) magnificent feast of simple foods: more bread, a covered pot of mashed beans, dates, and grapes, together with a couple of skins of water. As they shared the simple meal together, the young men began to relax and talk more freely; Shenoute even joked about needing to take second helpings as he tried on a tunic much too large for him.

Pachomius turned to the old man. "I don't understand," he told him. "We don't know you. You have no obligation to us or our families, and we don't have money to pay you. And yet you come to us in prison, you feed us, you clothe us. What are you getting out of this? Why are you doing it?"

The man smiled. "Because we're Christ's followers, my friend," he replied. "This is what we do."

ALL ABOUT LOVE

This was a transformative experience for Pachomius. On his release from the army he traveled back to Thebes to find the "Christ-followers" and was soon baptized. Looking for training in the way of life Jesus taught, he turned to the growing community of ascetics in the Egyptian desert and eventually founded a community further down the river at Tabennisi: a place where people could live together and learn the way of Christ with one another. It was one of the earliest monastic communities in Egypt and became a model for similar institutions across the Middle East and Europe; by the time of his death, Pachomius had founded eight communities consisting of several hundred monks.

All this flowed from a simple act of gracious, generous love, and it was this same love that Pachomius sought to nurture in his monasteries. All the prayer, work, study, service, silence, and obedience of the monks was designed to create the perfect environment for love to flourish: a deep and abiding love of God, and a wholehearted, overflowing love for one another. Pachomius understood that loving community was the natural outworking of a God-soaked life.

More than a millennium and a half later, another prisoner found himself sharing Pachomius's reflections on love and community. Imprisoned in a concentration camp for resistance to the Nazi regime, the German pastor Dietrich Bonhoeffer spent much of his time caring for fellow prisoners and leading them in simple acts of prayer and worship. Some years before he had come to learn the value of loving community while running an underground seminary in Finkenwalde. Reflecting on those years of shared life, he later wrote:

> It is true, of course, that what is an unspeakable gift of God for the lonely individual is easily disregarded and trodden under foot by those who have the gift every day. . . . [The community] is a gift of grace, a gift of the Kingdom of God that any day may

be taken from us. . . . It is grace, nothing but grace, that we are allowed to live in community.

It's not surprising to discover that Jesus also placed love at the very heart of his teaching about how to live in response to the in-breaking kingdom of God, the immanent God-soaked community he had come to herald. It is without doubt the clearest and most prominent leitmotif throughout all his sermons, sayings, and conversations: he constantly speaks either directly of love itself or of the manifestation of love in grace, mercy, justice, forgiveness, kindness, and reconciliation in the relationships people share with one another and with God.

With every passing year I find myself thinking, reflecting, meditating, writing, and preaching more and more about love. My wife sometimes jokes that I only have one sermon these days. I'll start to tell her about visiting one of the hundreds of churches I serve as spirituality adviser in my diocese. "I already know what you told them," she'll say, laughing: "God loves you!" And she's right. Mind you, if you're going to get stuck on one message, I can think of worse ones. The apostle John, in his nineties, used to be carried into the church in Ephesus on a stretcher to preach. His message, we're told, was also always the same: "Little children, love one another." When one of the younger church members complained, asking him to talk about something else for a change, John simply replied, "But this is what the Lord taught us to do. This one thing alone—this is *enough*."

John had heard this firsthand. "I give you a new commandment," Jesus told his disciples over a meal the night of his arrest in Jerusalem, "that you love one another. Just as I have loved you, you also should love one another" (John 13:34-35). And he gave this "new commandment" immediately after kneeling before them, one after another, and washing their feet before the meal: in ancient societies, the task of the lowest slave. "I have set you an example," he then said, "that you also should do as I have done to you" (John 13:15). It was clear that this "new commandment" to love would find practical expression in deep humility and acts of profound service. Self-giving love would be the hallmark of the kingdom.

LOVE'S LIMITS

The love Jesus proclaimed extended far beyond any immediate community. The primary calling would always be to love God "with all your heart, and with all your soul, and with all your mind, and with all your strength," that is, with the totality of our being. But a derivative, and equally important, calling followed it: "You shall love your neighbor as yourself" (Mark 12:30-31). And the concept of "neighbor" proved to be very broad indeed in Jesus' teaching. Jesus was asked on one occasion by a Scripture scholar: "Who is my neighbor?" In response, Jesus told a story in which a traveler, beaten and left for dead beside the road to Jerusalem, was ignored by both a passing priest and a Levite, representatives of the devout Jewish worshiping community. But shortly after, a Samaritan—a member of an ethnic community despised and reviled by Jews—stopped to provide a remarkable level of assistance, showing the deepest and most generous love.

At the end of the story Jesus neatly recast the issue at stake. Rather than asking, "Who is your neighbor?" he turned the tables on the scholar and asked, "Which of these three, do you think, *was a neighbor*?" (Luke 10:29-37, emphasis added). In other words, rather than asking who qualified as a neighbor, Jesus invited his listeners to consider who needed a neighbor, and what kind of neighbor they themselves could be. Love suddenly became a very broad roof under which people might shelter.

As if to underline the point, Jesus shocked his listeners by bluntly insisting: "Love your enemies and pray for those who persecute you.... For if you love those who love you, what reward do you have? ... And if you greet only your brothers and sisters, what more are you doing than others?" (Matthew 5:44-47). The love that characterized the kingdom of God, then, was to be extended to all regardless of whether or not they reciprocated. Jesus expected his followers to love their families and kin, their difficult neighbors, their closest friends, and their most bitter opponents. Even in the face of death they were expected to emulate his grace and forgiveness, seen in his prayer for his executioners while dying on the cross: "Father, forgive them; for they do not know what they are doing" (Luke 23:34).

There is a startling profligacy to this love. Jesus taught his disciples to love their friends, their neighbors, and their enemies. He welcomed the company of religious leaders and social outcasts, of priests and prostitutes, of Roman soldiers and the members of the resistance who fought them. He touched lepers, scandalized his peers by keeping company with immoral women, and feasted with sinners. His hospitality seemed limitless.

And that's a love and hospitality we can experience too—sometimes in ways that surprise us. I can still vividly remember the first day I arrived at a church of the homeless that I was part of for a year in the early nineties. Within minutes of turning up I found myself sitting over lunch with some of the most varied and interesting company I'd kept in years: Jock, the elderly alcoholic; Michelle, an addict and sex worker; Doug, who dealt on the street corner to support his own habit; Alec, on day release from the local open prison; and a handful of others whose lives revolved around the streets, their addictions, and the gaping wounds in their histories and characters.

I remember thinking, as I sat at the table, *This is such a gift and opportunity. I can be Jesus to these people. I can show them his love, his generosity of spirit, his hospitality. I can help make Christ real here.* So I set out to be as open, loving, and gracious as possible, to reflect something of Jesus' character in that place.

It was weeks before I really understood what was going on. During a short service one lunchtime someone read one of Jesus' most striking stories from Matthew's Gospel. On the last day, Jesus said, every nation will be gathered into his presence and separated into two groups, "as a shepherd separates the sheep from the goats." He described himself turning to one group and welcoming them into the "kingdom prepared for you from the foundation of the world"—the God-soaked community of love that has been God's purpose and passion from all eternity. They'll be welcomed, Jesus said, because "I was hungry and you gave me food, I was thirsty and you gave me something to drink, I was a stranger and you welcomed me, I was naked and you gave me clothing, I was sick and you took care of me, I was in prison and you visited me." I couldn't help thinking, as the story was being read: *That's us! That's what we're doing here: helping the hungry, thirsty, and homeless; caring for the sick and lost; even occasionally visiting people in prison! We're living this gospel story!* It was a good feeling.

Then the reader carried on; Jesus described the puzzled crowd questioning him: "When was it that we saw you hungry and gave you food, or thirsty and gave you something to drink? When did we see you a stranger, naked, sick, or imprisoned, and cared for you?" And Jesus responded simply, "Just as you did it for one of the least of these who are members of my family, you did it to me" (Matthew 25:31-40).

And then it hit me, immediately and with all the power of a lightning strike. I wasn't Jesus in that place: *they were*. These addicts, alcoholics, street girls, dealers, and rough sleepers were Jesus. I wasn't showering them with the beneficent love of Jesus (lucky them!)—I was being invited into the divine presence. I was experiencing the extraordinary hospitality of Christ that turns the world on its head.

It was an important lesson in the love found in God's kingdom. Apprentices in the God-soaked life don't start by showing love and hospitality, they start by being loved and welcomed, by discovering Christ in the people who surround them, especially the most damaged and troubled. And when they find in them the depth of Christ's love and welcome, they learn in turn how to love well, how to open their lives to others. Love is our hallmark, and we find it in the faces and lives of the poor, the broken, and the lost.

THE GREAT
COMMISSION

Jesus expected this unbounded, ever-open love to be the hallmark of his followers. "By this everyone will know that you are my disciples, if you have love for one another" (John 13:35). But Jesus' followers seem always to have found it challenging to keep love at the center of their lives and communities. A reading of the history of Christ's followers across the last two thousand years reveals much to celebrate in this regard: deacons caring for widows and orphans; friars living among the poor and outcast; reformers challenging the slave trade or appalling prison conditions; campaigners bringing debt relief to the world's most impoverished nations. But there is also much to lament: horrific inquisitions against heretics, pogroms against Jews, crusades unleashing violence across the Middle East and beyond, persecution of minorities into the present day. It is beguilingly easy, apparently, to rationalize away the costly call to love in favor of actions closer to our own interests.

In this regard it's fascinating to observe how, over the last century or so, many people have placed enormous weight on an alternative characteristic of Jesus' kingdom community highlighted in a passage from Matthew's Gospel widely known as the Great Commission:

All authority in heaven and on earth has been given to me. Go therefore and make disciples of all nations, baptizing them in the name of the Father and of the Son and of the Holy Spirit, and teaching them to obey everything that I have commanded you. (Matthew 28:18-20)

In Matthew's narrative of Jesus' life these are the words he speaks to his disciples shortly before returning to the Father's presence. By the late nineteenth century they were heavily emphasized by the burgeoning missionary movement as Jesus' final—and therefore most pressing—instruction. At a hugely influential conference at Mount Vernon in 1886, one speaker issued a challenge to the congregation: "Show, if you can, why you should not obey the last command of Jesus Christ!" And mission was increasingly seen as obedience to this "last command": the hugely influential Dutch statesman and church founder Abraham Kuyper once said, "All mission flows from God's sovereignty, not from God's love or compassion." The message was clear: it's not about love, it's about doing what Jesus has told us to do.

In our time this missionary impulse born of obedience to Jesus' commandment has increasingly been viewed as the central and defining quality that should be evident in all communities of Christ's followers. Those who claim to have placed Christ at the center of their lives must above all, it is often asserted, be those who reach out with the message of Christ to others.

This reading of the Gospel has been far-reaching in its influence. It has fueled countless movements, inspired missionaries around the world, and shaped the lives of individuals and communities. It has led to an outpouring of books, magazines, pamphlets, movies, radio programs, television and Internet shows, plays, songs, and endless other artistic and media-centered attempts to explain the story and significance of Jesus to as wide an audience as possible. It has even shaped the way Christ-followers have thought and talked about God, casting God in an essentially missionary role in creation and history, and finding the identity of the kingdom community in its participation in that mission.

WHAT MATTERED TO JESUS

In the light of such an enthusiastic and widespread expenditure of time and energy, it's somewhat sobering to discover that Jesus himself never placed this missionary impulse at the center of his teaching about the kingdom, nor did he ever use the term *Great Commission* to describe those closing words of Matthew's Gospel.

Surprisingly, Jesus often *discouraged* people from talking about him and about his message. On one occasion after another he pressed people to keep the gospel message to themselves. "He sternly ordered the disciples not to tell anyone that he was the Messiah" (Matthew 16:20). After healing a leper, Jesus said to him, "See that you say nothing to anyone" (Matthew 8:4). Jesus raised a young girl from the dead, then "strictly ordered [those present] that no one should know this" (Mark 5:43). Following the healing of a deaf man, Jesus turned to the crowd and "ordered them to tell no one" (Mark 7:36). Speaking to Peter, James, and John after he revealed his glory on the mountain, he "ordered them to tell no one about what they had seen, until after the Son of Man had risen from the dead" (Mark 9:9). Recognized by evil spirits he was confronting, "he rebuked them and would not allow them to speak, because they knew that he was the Messiah" (Luke 4:41). Asked by the disciples why he taught in parables, he quoted the book of Isaiah: "so that 'looking they may not perceive, and listening they may not understand'" (Luke 8:10).

In one curious episode in John's Gospel, Jesus' brothers encourage him to attend a festival in Jerusalem, since "no one who wants to be widely known acts in secret." Jesus refuses, telling them it's the wrong time for him to act publicly there. But John then reports that "after his brothers had gone to the festival, then he also went, not publicly but as it were in secret" (John 7:1-10). Whatever we make of these (and similar) incidents individually, it's hard to read them cumulatively as evidence that preaching, speaking, and talking about Jesus is the defining characteristic of a kingdom community.

This secrecy of Jesus has puzzled readers and scholars of the Gospels through the centuries; of course, if you assume that Jesus' message is a missionary message in its very essence, it becomes not simply puzzling but outright inexplicable. Is Jesus only discouraging people from talking about him during his years of preaching and teaching, a prohibition that is overturned after the events of the first Easter when the meaning of his words and actions will become clear? Or is he, perhaps, trying to hold back those who haven't made a concrete decision to follow him, those who have simply been beneficiaries of his healing gifts? Or is it some kind of reverse psychology: by insisting people don't talk about him, he more or less guarantees that they will?

That last possibility reminds me of the delightful story of a man who, having come to faith in Christ, was encouraged to share his new faith as widely as possible but found himself paralyzed by fear at the prospect. He tried in a dozen different ways to talk about Christ with his friends and neighbors, but always found himself struck mute with anxiety at the crucial moment. So he went to see his pastor to discuss the problem. The pastor, a wise and experienced minister, regarded him thoughtfully for a moment before replying, "My friend, in normal circumstances it would be necessary for you to talk about your faith at every opportunity. But I sense that, in your case, there should be a dispensation. I feel as though the Lord is saying very clearly to you: you never have to talk about me to anyone, ever." The man was delighted, so relieved to be rid of his crippling burden. He ran straight home, burst into his living room, and proclaimed joyfully to his wife: "Honey, I have wonderful news! I've given my life to Jesus—and I never have to tell anyone about it!"

THE REAL COMMISSION

Jesus did, however, explicitly offer another "Great Commission" around which his entire understanding of God's kingdom crystallized and found its identity. If we understand a *commission* as an "instruction or command to act in a particular manner" then Jesus clearly identified his Great Commission on more than one occasion. Mark's Gospel, for example, describes a conversation between Jesus and a Scripture scholar (known as a "scribe"):

> One of the scribes ... asked him, "Which commandment is the first of all?" Jesus answered, "The first is, 'Hear, O Israel: the Lord our God, the Lord is one; you shall love the Lord your God with all your heart, and with all your soul, and with all your mind, and with all your strength.' The second is this, 'You shall love your neighbor as yourself.' There is no other commandment greater than these." Then the scribe said to him, "You are right, Teacher; you have truly said that 'he is one, and beside him there is no other'; and 'to love him with all the heart, and with all the understanding, and with all the strength,' and 'to love one's neighbor as oneself,'—this is much more important than all whole burnt offerings and sacrifices." When Jesus saw that he answered wisely, he said to him, "You are not far from the kingdom of God." (Mark 12:28-34)

Listen to those last words again. "Not far from the kingdom of God." The only remaining step for this scholar, perhaps, was to translate the idea into action, to come to learn from experience that "on these two commandments hang all the law and the prophets" (Matthew 22:40); that is (as the apostle Paul, another Scripture scholar, put it): "the one who loves another has fulfilled the law" (Romans 13:8).

At its heart, the kingdom of God is not a missionary community that loves. It is a loving community that reaches out beyond itself. Faithful followers of Jesus don't love people in order to share the good news about Jesus with them. They love people, period. One of the ways they love is by sharing good news, but love is always the end, and other outreach activities always the means to that end. Love always has the primacy, love is always the goal.

A twentieth-century Swiss writer, Emil Brunner, once said, "The church exists by mission as a fire exists by burning. Where there is no mission, there is no church." It's a stirring and evocative line. But it simply doesn't echo the priorities of Jesus, who clearly and repeatedly placed love—love for God, for one another, for neighbor, and for enemies—at the very center of the life of God's kingdom community. Almost every line of the gospel seems to say, rather, "The church exists by love as a fire exists by burning. Where there is no love, there is no church." Whatever we understand by the idea of "mission," it has to be seen as an expression of our primary vocation to love. It is never an absolute in the God-soaked life, never superior to the life of love.

In the end, it's sobering to wonder how the last century or so of history might have looked if we'd read the gospel differently. To consider what would have happened if the world's millions of followers of Jesus had taken all the passion, time, and energy that went into seeking converts and poured it instead into the simple and painful business of doing what Jesus actually did and taught his followers to do: loving people who may never love them back.

LEARNING LOVE
IN GENTLENESS

THE CALL TO LOVE IS VAST: rooted in the very structuring of creation, encompassing everything that lives and breathes, summoning us to give our uttermost to God and one another. But, as with so many other essential aspects of our lives, it begins small and often finds expression in the most seemingly mundane ways.

If we want to learn the great art of love from Jesus, we might begin by being attentive to the many small acts of gentleness, kindness, and courtesy that graced his most ordinary interactions with other people. It's easy to miss these, overshadowed as they often are by his astounding miracles and provocative pronouncements. But once we begin to look for them, we discover them over and over again: natural, instinctive, spontaneous expressions of tenderness that make love manifest in small but significant ways.

Think, for example, of Mark's story about Jesus healing a leper:

A leper came to him begging him, and kneeling he said to him, "If you choose, you can make me clean." Moved with pity, Jesus stretched out his hand and touched him, and said to him, "I do choose. Be made clean!" Immediately the leprosy left him, and he was made clean. (Mark 1:40-42)

The healing itself is dramatic and very much the centerpiece of the narrative. But what always catches my attention is that brief moment

in the middle where Jesus "stretched out his hand and touched him."
Just take a moment to reflect what that might have meant. His skin
disease not only afflicted him physically but also socially, relationally.
This illness made him unclean, a pariah and outcast, unable to participate in community life. The book of Leviticus provided that

> the person who has the leprous disease shall wear torn clothes
> and let the hair of his head be disheveled; and he shall cover his
> upper lip and cry out, "Unclean, unclean." He shall remain un-
> clean as long as he has the disease; he is unclean. He shall live
> alone; his dwelling shall be outside the camp. (Leviticus 13:45-46)

Leviticus also taught that the state of being "unclean" was easily
acquired (simply brushing your clothing against an unclean person in
the street could be sufficient) but hard to remove; ritual cleansing
would mean washing or bathing, perhaps sacrifices and ceremonies,
and sometimes a period of time in isolation. In some cases, unclean
objects would even need to be destroyed; clay pots would be shattered (Leviticus 11:33) and infected houses could be torn down
(Leviticus 14:45). Ritual cleanliness was taken extremely seriously.

It's hardly surprising, then, that the man's request to Jesus was not
simply "heal me" but, more importantly, "make me clean." His longing
for simple human interaction—to sit beside someone, to hold a hand,
to embrace his parents or (perhaps) hold his children—would have
been intense. So notice again Jesus' *first* reaction to the man's request.
Not to teach. Not to console. Not even to heal. "Moved with pity," we
are told, Jesus *touches* him.

The miracle that followed was an act of divine power. But the touch
is pure kindness, an act of beautiful divine tenderness. Imagine what
that touch meant to the leper: acceptance, recognition of his dignity,
simple human warmth.

For Jesus, this was no isolated incident. When confronted with
suffering and isolated human beings he seemed instinctively to want

to reach out and touch them, to gently restore them into human community. Finding Peter's mother-in-law sick with a fever he "touched her hand," which led to her healing (Matthew 8:15). Two blind men come to him looking for healing, and he "touched their eyes" (Matthew 9:29). A synagogue leader's twelve-year-old daughter died; Jesus came and "took her by the hand" (Luke 8:54). When he witnessed a widow leading her son's funeral procession out of the town of Nain, he "came forward and touched the bier" before raising the young man back to life (Luke 7:14). When a woman suffering from internal bleeding reaches out and touches him, he calls on her to publicly identify herself, not so he can chastise her, unclean as she was, for daring to touch the holy robes of the rabbi, but so he can publicly declare her well and so end her ostracism (Luke 8:47-48). Jesus repeatedly used the small courtesies of touch to reassure, to console, to acknowledge, to comfort.

THE ART OF DISTRACTION

Perhaps, though, the most moving story of Jesus' courtesy in action is found in the story of the woman caught in the act of adultery, related in the eighth chapter of John's Gospel. It's easy to picture the scene. The woman, terrified and confused, was dragged through the streets into the precincts of the temple and thrown into the midst of a crowd gathered around Jesus. Angry voices demanded her execution by stoning. The atmosphere was surely tense, her fate balanced on a knife edge. And what did Jesus do? He "bent down and wrote with his finger on the ground." They keep pressing him for an answer; he suggests that the one without sin should begin the stoning. Then "once again he bent down and wrote on the ground" (John 8:6, 8).

What in the world was he doing? Lakes of commentators' ink have been spilled over this puzzling and vexed question. Was he, as some suggest, writing a list of the sins of those present, a counterpoint to his invitation for those who believed themselves sinless to stone the woman? Was he writing words from Scripture? With consummate ingenuity, some scholars have tried to calculate the number of Hebrew letters that could be written in the dirt, given the minimum size of legible letter and the maximum reach of Jesus' hand while crouching down (based on the unexplained assumption that he didn't shift position as he wrote), leading to the inescapable conclusion that it was a line from Jeremiah. Or Deuteronomy. Or Leviticus. Or some other biblical book. Perhaps, say others, he was writing the names of those present, or the Ten Words from Sinai, or . . . the list is almost endless.

For two thousand years people have wondered over those words in the sand. And so, in one brief action, Jesus captured the attention of the crowd around him and of every reader of the Gospel in the centuries to follow. And the result, curiously, is that the terrified and exposed woman dragged into public view at the beginning of the story slips quietly into the shadows. I can't help but wonder: was this Jesus' intention all along? Perhaps his bending down to write was nothing more than his kindness at work, drawing their gaze (and ours) away from her and toward him. If so, it was a startlingly effective gambit. By the end of the story, everyone has left and the woman is unharmed. And Jesus—the only person to speak to her directly—has offered her grace and forgiveness. Hauled into the narrative without dignity and in mortal danger, she walks away at the end free, forgiven, and at peace. Kindness and courtesy can be unexpectedly powerful.

The opportunities for us to practice gentleness and kindness in our day-to-day lives, to give other people the gift of dignity and significance, are manifold; they present themselves to us almost constantly. Every interaction and conversation opens up the potential for us to share—and receive—grace. Rather than choosing only between driving aggressively or defensively, we can opt to drive generously and courteously. In the bank, at the store, around the office, in the street with strangers, or at home with family, we can challenge the normal patterns of behavior we too often see and, perhaps, indulge in ourselves:

withdrawn, self-absorbed, goal focused, hurried, protective. Instead we can seek to be more open, warm, engaged, outward looking.

We might even want to practice the marvelous spiritual discipline of being polite. How sad it is that even the *idea* of being polite is suspect in some quarters! We see people seasoning their lives with small gestures and pleasantries, holding open doors and offering seats on a crowded bus, greeting strangers and wishing one another a nice day. And in our age, which prizes authenticity so highly, we question the sincerity of these little moments: Do you think I'm unable to stand for this journey? Do you think a friendly hello makes us friends? Do you really want me to have a nice day? Under the weight of our fierce questioning it all appears so hollow and trite. So we drop the social graces, withdraw into our authentic selves, and present ourselves to the world as we truly are: wary, angry, gloomy, or aggressive, whatever mood we find ourselves in each day. And all the while never asking ourselves: What if I simply took these pleasantries and *made* them sincere? Decided to show warmth, regardless of my own changing temperament? Chose to wish you well as an act of love, however small? What if my choice, like that of Jesus, were always to give myself a little to the person right in front of me, to touch them, to give them worth, regardless of who they are and how they are behaving toward me? That is the great and hidden power of courtesy—and Jesus was a master.

RELATIONSHIPS MADE WHOLE

Courtesy builds love; reconciliation repairs it. The need for forgiveness emerges when kindness breaks down, when that recognition of another's dignity and worth, which fuels courtesy, has been lost. Even in communities aspiring to love well, frictions arise, tempers fray, and mistakes are made. When love is pushed into second place, made a means toward other ends, or neglected altogether, malice and betrayal flourish and the need for reconciliation between individuals, families, and larger social groups (sometimes even nations) becomes ever more urgent.

Jesus treated this matter of the healing of relationships with the utmost seriousness, which is hardly surprising when we understand the kingdom he announced and embodied as a community of love above all else. His words on the subject in his famous Sermon on the Mount, the seminal teaching found in the early chapters of Matthew's Gospel, are trenchant and direct:

> You have heard that it was said to those of ancient times, "You shall not murder"; and "whoever murders shall be liable to judgment." But I say to you that if you are angry with a brother or sister, you will be liable to judgment; and if you insult a brother or sister, you will be liable to the council; and if you say, "You fool," you will be liable to the hell of fire. So when you are offering your gift at the altar, if you remember that your brother or sister has something against you, leave your gift there before the altar and go; first be reconciled to your brother or sister, and then come and offer your gift. (Matthew 5:21-24)

Having asserted that even the smallest infraction against love—an insult or angry word—is a matter of great import, and that it is better to leave sacrifices unoffered than to leave broken relationships unhealed, Jesus went on to highlight some of the ways we most commonly break faith with one another: through adultery and betrayal in marriage, by breaking our verbal commitments, by retaliating vindictively when subjected to violence or imposition. And he summed this up with his call to show indiscriminate love to all, regardless of their behavior toward us, to love neighbor, friend, stranger, and enemy with equal alacrity. "Be perfect," he concluded, "as your heavenly Father is perfect" (Matthew 5:48).

This was not primarily a call to complete moral perfection but, in the context, should rather be understood as an urging to show wholehearted love to one another. That's a theme which recurs throughout the Gospels. In the eighteenth chapter of Matthew, for example, we find three conversations, one after another, exploring the extent of reconciliation and forgiveness that Jesus' followers are expected to offer. Jesus discussed the process of challenging destructive behavior within the community, setting out the guidance that the offender should be offered every opportunity to make amends in private, with a small group of friends, even in the face of the whole community, before any decision is made that their actions are simply too disruptive to be contained with the community (Matthew 18:15-20). Peter then asked how often he should personally forgive someone who hurts him: seven times? Jesus' reply was expansive: "Not seven times, but, I tell you, seventy-seven times." Which, unless Peter was going to keep tremendously careful records, was effectively the same as saying: never stop forgiving (Matthew 18:21-22). Then Jesus offered a story about a servant forgiven an astonishing and crippling debt who immediately finds one of his peers and tries to squeeze him for a handful of coins; Jesus was scathing about the man's behavior and clearly intended his disciples to reflect on the boundless grace they themselves, in their weaknesses and failure, had received from God before turning in anger on their fallible and broken neighbors (Matthew 18:23-34).

Forgiveness and reconciliation are not easy. That needs to be acknowledged openly and freely. It is often glib and unhelpful simply to urge one another to "forgive and forget." To let go of minor slights and unintended hurts is, perhaps, a straightforward matter. But many of us have received serious and bitter wounds at one another's hands; we have been neglected and disappointed, betrayed and abused, sometimes maliciously savaged. And those who have wounded us frequently show little or no remorse, no desire to work with us to mend the relationship; they may even celebrate their vicious behavior. Forgiveness is *hard*. But then, much of the kingdom life Jesus described is hard. He spoke of self-denial, of putting the kingdom ahead of our most cherished loved ones, of taking up the cross (an instrument of suffering and torture), of being ready to lay down our lives.

The question we should be asking is not, is it hard? It is. The crucial question is, which is harder? To persist in unforgiveness, as the bitter cancer of fury and regret eats away at our soul, corrodes all our relationships with God and other people, destroys any sense of self-worth, consumes us with sorrow and darkness? Or to make a different and also difficult choice: to love, despite all? This, in the end, is the challenging way toward abundance of life. No wonder that Jesus warned his disciples, "The gate is narrow and the way is hard that leads to life, and there are few who find it" (Matthew 7:14). Nevertheless, lead to life it surely does.

OVER TO YOU

Scripture and Reflection

IN THESE PAGES WE'VE TALKED ABOUT the way that love for God naturally overflows into love for one another and creates community. We've seen that this profligate and ever-expanding love is the hallmark of a kingdom people and can be seen in the life of Jesus in numerous ways. We considered the gracious love seen in Jesus' many small acts of gentleness and kindness, and the rather more challenging call of Jesus for us to seek reconciliation in the midst of broken relationships.

Here again are some readings and questions that may help you reflect on these ideas. If you find that some of them are especially helpful in stimulating your own thinking and prayer, stick with those. Alternatively, you might find it helpful to work through the daily readings over the coming week.

- *Matthew 25:31–46*

    How does this parable shape your understanding of what it means to follow Jesus? Does it challenge or console you?

- *Ephesians 4:1-3*

    Where have you come closest to experiencing the kind of community Paul describes here? What was it like?

- *1 Corinthians 13*

   How does this well-known passage inform or test the ideas we've explored in this chapter?

- *John 20:21-23*

   How might these words of Jesus affect our understanding of our "mission"? What do they tell us about our calling to love God and one another?

- *Luke 8:40-56*

   How are the gentleness, kindness, and courtesy of Jesus revealed in this story? How important do you think they are? What can we learn here?

- *Matthew 5:43-48*

   Are there limits to who we should love? Do you find it easy to love your enemies? How might we learn to love those we find hard to love?

- *Matthew 18:15-20*

   How do you deal with conflict and reconciliation in the communities you live in? How might Jesus' teaching help you or challenge you?

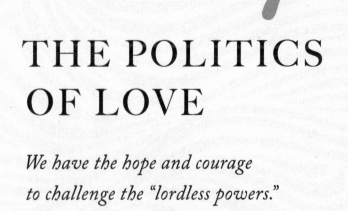

THE POLITICS OF LOVE

We have the hope and courage to challenge the "lordless powers."

AGAINST THE DARKNESS

GLORIOUS POSSIBILITIES

THE KINGDOM TODAY

OVER TO YOU

AGAINST THE
DARKNESS

COOKING WITH ANTOINE was always an educational experience. In his youth Antoine had been a Cordon Bleu chef; I knew that because he told me. Repeatedly. When we met he was responsible for providing a daily hot meal at the church of the homeless where I also found myself for a year, and one of my first assignments there was to work as his assistant.

Admittedly our resources were pretty basic. One domestic oven and hob, a handful of donated pans, some knives and spatulas that had seen better days. And for ingredients, outdated fruit and vegetables from a local supermarket, together with surplus tinned foods from the nearby warehouse of a European Union refugee program. The cans, a mixture of processed meats, beans, sliced fruits, and soups, all had one peculiar feature in common: no labels.

With Antoine in charge, that was unimportant. His recipe and method were unchanged from one day to the next. Place the largest saucepan on the hob. Open roughly one tin per two people and empty the contents into the pan; minced beef, apricots, chicken soup, haricot beans, sardines—it didn't matter what came out, it all got mixed in together. Then chop and slice all the fresh food (usually my job), the lettuce and onions, mushrooms, and kiwi fruit. Everything. That all got tossed in the pan too. Finally, heat the pan to within an inch of its life, simmer for an hour until mushy, then serve with bread and hot tea.

I found myself reassessing my idea of cordon bleu. But most members of that church, like Antoine, were homeless. Their daily lives were a mixture of rough sleeping, addiction issues, tangling with the authorities, dodging violent assaults, and scraping together enough cash to keep themselves warm and fed. Antoine's ghastly bowls of sludge were hot, filling, calorie laden, and most importantly *free*. We rarely had any complaints.

Cooking with Antoine was my introduction to the world of politics. Until I first walked into that kitchen, I'd thought politics was about manifestos and elections, demonstrations and protests, focus groups and sound bites. But over that huge, hot saucepan I discovered politics of a more raw and earthy form, closer to the original sense of the word. Antoine's kitchen was an outworking of the shape of our wider *polis*, our community and society.

Here I began to see for myself that politics touches lives. We had a system of governance, a way of structuring our communities and making decisions together, which had formed a particular political reality; this reality shaped all our lives to some degree, for good or for ill. That reality had, among other things, created that kitchen.

It was the beginning of an education for me, a slow process of learning that politics is not, in the end, about parties and allegiances, nor even about ideas, economics, or the forces of history. It is about people: rich and poor, women and men, old and young, powerful and marginalized. It was an important step for me in coming to understand how Jesus' teaching about the kingdom, about a loving community centered on the presence of God, affects the way we live in our wider society. I was learning a profound lesson about the politics of Jesus.

REVOLUTIONARY JESUS

It's tempting, of course, to see Jesus as an entirely apolitical figure. He didn't found, join, endorse, or even talk about any political party. He never stood for any public office or role in government. People sometimes make enthusiastic efforts to project back onto Jesus the issues and opinions of our own times, but his life and teaching simply don't fit neatly into the left and right world of contemporary politics. Jesus said nothing about welfare payments, health care, educational policy, or international relations. He had no fiscal policy or economic philosophy to offer. He wasn't a capitalist, conservative, liberal, socialist, communist, or freethinker—no matter how much we wish he were! The Gospels simply don't allow us to squeeze him into these modern boxes.

In 1999 the Churches Advertising Network in the United Kingdom ran a controversial and provocative publicity campaign. They put up hundreds of posters and distributed thousands of leaflets with an image of Christ created by blending a movie still of Jesus with Jim Fitzpatrick's iconic photo portrait of Che Guevara.

The backlash was immediate and fierce. Public figures and newspapers weighed in to suggest that the image was "blasphemous" and "sacrilegious." One politician called for the excommunication of the advertisers. By far the fiercest response came from political conservatives, which raised an interesting question: was the great offense identifying Jesus with a violent revolutionary, or identifying Jesus with the political left?

But the real issue was deeper still. The *Washington Post*, watching from across the pond, nailed what for many was the key problem with the campaign: the idea that Jesus would have any kind of politics at all. They branded the whole affair "symptomatic of a silliness that respects no borders" and called it a "displacement of dignity by merchandising that trivializes." And then they asked the crucial question: "In what sense was Jesus, who said 'My kingdom is not of this world,' political?"

ON THE PUBLIC STAGE

It's a great question—all the more so when you realize that, oddly, Jesus was seen as a significant political figure in his own society from the moment of his birth. His coming into the world sent ripples through the entire political establishment. According to the Gospel writers he was visited in his infancy by a group of *magi*, royal ambassadors from the East, whose astrological charts predicted that he would become king (Matthew 2:2-12). Herod the Great, the bloodthirsty and tyrannical king in Jerusalem, responded by trying to assassinate the newborn usurper; he slaughtered all the children in Bethlehem, and Joseph and Mary were forced into exile in Egypt (Matthew 2:13-15).

Jesus launched his public life some three decades later by identifying himself with John the Baptist, a prophet whose message had a sharp social edge: "Whoever has two coats must share with anyone who has none," he taught; "and whoever has food must do likewise" (Luke 3:11). John challenged tax collectors and Roman soldiers, and eventually found himself imprisoned and executed because he spoke out publicly against the immorality of Herod Antipas, son of Herod the Great (Mark 6:17-29).

Jesus' own message was incendiary. It's worth hearing the words again: "The time is fulfilled, and the kingdom of God has come near; repent, and believe in the good news" (Mark 1:15). Jesus was relativizing the authority of all human government: the power of the Herodian dynasty in Galilee, the Roman governor in Judea, the religious council of the Sanhedrin in Jerusalem, even Caesar ruling from his distant throne in Rome. The kingdom of God is a seditious and subversive proclamation.

And Jesus wasn't slow to spell out the social implications of God's kingdom. Before his first public sermon in Nazareth, Jesus read briefly from the scroll of the prophet Isaiah:

> The Spirit of the Lord is upon me,
>   because he has anointed me
>   to bring good news to the poor.
> He has sent me to proclaim release to the captives
>   and recovery of sight to the blind,
>   to let the oppressed go free,
> to proclaim the year of the Lord's favor.

Then Jesus handed back the scroll and bluntly announced, "Today this scripture has been fulfilled in your hearing" (Luke 4:16-21). This was how Jesus thought and spoke about the kingdom of God: a place of liberation, release, and good news for the poor.

A DIFFICULT LEGACY

It was no accident that Jesus went back to the prophet Isaiah to find words to express his kingdom vision. From beginning to end the Hebrew Bible shines with the vision of a loving, redemptive, and deeply human society. The ancient Jewish writers lived in an era in which poverty was endemic, violence was widespread, brutality was the language of power, and the struggle to survive dominated the lives of many ordinary people. And yet they were inspired by the dream of a community of loving people with God himself at its very heart—what Jesus would later call the kingdom of God—and by the hope that this dream could be made real in their own lives.

Certainly this vision could be expressed in some strange and disturbing ways. The Israelites were trying to realize God's kingdom community in a society that was profoundly and unthinkingly different from our own, a society marked by deeply unequal relationships between men and women, by slavery, by ferocious and bloody legal punishments. So we find that cursing your parents is a capital offense (Exodus 21:17), that those who practice other religions are to be stoned to death (Deuteronomy 17:2-5), and that a rapist can make amends to society for his crime by marrying his victim (Deuteronomy 22:28-29).

We might want to try to explain, reconcile, or defend the Bible when we read these passages. But I think we need to find the courage to be honest: for us, at least, these kinds of provisions are bizarre, incomprehensible, and abhorrent. That's a problem for us as we try to discern God's voice speaking through Scripture, but we need to keep reminding ourselves that we are listening to voices from another world and another age as they wrestle, sometimes

well and sometimes poorly, with the possibilities the
kingdom presents.

My grandfather, a Methodist local preacher and delightfully devout
man, lived in a generation that was characterized by pervasive dis-
crimination against women and an ugly casual racism that permeated
every community. Did he challenge that? Not as far as I'm aware: he
shared a widespread cultural blindness about these issues (I, in turn,
share the blindnesses of *my* culture). But he was still a holy and beautiful man, and I make him no less holy when I acknowledge the shortcomings of his time.

It's the same with the Bible. We don't make the Bible's vision of
society any less glorious and compelling when we admit that it comes
to us filtered through the lens of a flawed culture. Parts of the Bible
are difficult. Let's simply admit that.

But that's not the whole picture.

GLORIOUS
POSSIBILITIES

SCRIPTURE CAN BE DARK AND DIFFICULT. Often, when I'm leading training sessions on praying with the Bible, I ask people to begin by coming up with word pictures to describe their present experience of the Bible. I start them off with a couple of very different examples from Scripture itself: a sharp, two-edged sword (Hebrews 4:12) and a lamp lighting the path (Psalm 119:105). Then I encourage folks to come up with their own original images. I've had some fabulous offerings over the years. "For me, the Bible is like a jack-in-the-box," said one person; "I wind the handle for ages and nothing happens—and then out something comes, *wham!* right between the eyes!" Another compared Scripture to an elderly uncle sleeping in the corner of the living room, "full of wisdom, but not speaking to me." A third spoke of the Bible as a case of fine wines they were savoring, glass by glass, as they read around the different books.

I'll always remember one response, though. I asked for a word image, and after some thought one of the people present said, "For me, it's a horror movie." I asked why. "Because I keep finding myself drawn back, again and again, to the murders, the genocides, the rapes, the bloodshed—often in the name of God. I can't escape it; the horror of it all won't leave me. It makes it hard for me to read." And that, it seems to me, is a reasonable response to at least some of what the Bible offers us.

By and large, though, the difficult passages are the ones that run *with* the grain of their prevailing culture. The underlying assumptions they employ (for example, that women are little more than property or that slavery is perfectly acceptable but freedom of religion is an appalling evil) were simply the unquestioned attitudes of every society of the ancient world. That doesn't justify them or make them any easier to deal with. But it does set them in some kind of context: we need to understand that what seems so alien and terrible to us would have been quite unexceptionable to our ancestors. In many respects, the Bible is a book rooted in a particular time and place, reflecting that context in all its brilliance and awfulness.

That said, some really interesting music begins to be heard when we listen for those passages that run *against* the grain of their day—and it's exactly these passages that shape the later vision of the prophets and Jesus' proclamation of the kingdom of God. Behind its detailed provisions for everyday life in an ancient Near Eastern society, the Hebrew law envisions a community quite unlike anything the world had ever seen or imagined.

The essential character of the community is summed up in the opening sentence of the Ten Commandments: "I am the LORD your God, who brought you out of the land of Egypt, out of the house of slavery" (Exodus 20:2). This short verse identifies three key characteristics of the community God was inviting the Hebrews to discover and share. It was to be a community of *grace*, called into being as an act of love. It was to be a community of *innovation*, unlike every other nation around. And it was to be a community of *change*, where transformed people lived in radically new relationships with one another—no longer slaves under Pharaoh, but free men and women carried "out of the house of slavery."

A COMMUNITY OF GRACE

The new community dreamed of in the Hebrew Bible was, above all else, experienced as a *gift*. No one set out to create this new society;

there were no brainstorming sessions, focus groups, or planning meetings, no congresses, conventions, and constitutions. Like creation itself, this came seemingly out of the blue, unexpected and undeserved, straight from the hand of God.

Abraham was apparently just one of thousands of citizens in the ancient city of Ur when God first tapped him on the shoulder. Yet he found himself the recipient of God's unprovoking blessing and holding the promise that his family would become a blessing to the whole earth. And so began a story in which guidance, blessing, direction, and redemption flowed from one generation to the next, their mistakes and misdemeanors constantly overwhelmed by God-initiated generosity and love. In fact, it's remarkable how often Scripture seems almost to delight in the flaws of God's people, as though underlining the astonishing extent of God's kindness and love.

Of all the books in the Hebrew Bible perhaps Deuteronomy grasps this divine grace most fully and enthusiastically. "You are a people holy to the LORD your God," we read; "the LORD your God has chosen you out of all the peoples on earth to be his people, his treasured possession" (Deuteronomy 7:6). And it's this perspective that informs the whole re-presentation of the covenant that forms the heart of the book. "Although heaven and the heaven of heavens belong to the LORD your God, the earth with all that is in it, yet the LORD set his heart in love on your ancestors alone and chose you, their descendants after them, out of all the peoples" (Deuteronomy 10:14-15). It's clear that the life of the community is, above all else, received as a gift.

Communities of grace are uncommon, and always stand out when we discover them. In our time many people have found this remarkable gift of community in twelve-step groups such as Alcoholics Anonymous. People wash up at the door of these groups at their lowest ebb, their lives like shattered wreckage on a storm-ridden ocean. No one in this room full of strangers owes them anything: they have no claims or rights here. And they find (sometimes to their amazement) that the door stands open wide. They are welcomed in, just as they are. Where did these groups learn such life-changing, unconditional love? One of the founders, Dr. Robert Smith, recalled their earliest days: "It wasn't until 1938 that the teachings and efforts and stories that had been going on were crystallized in the form of the Twelve Steps. . . . We already had the basic ideas, though not in terse and tangible form. We got them, as I said, as a result of our study of the Good Book."

FEARLESS INNOVATION

God offered the Israelites a vision of a new community visibly different than that of surrounding nations, a community removed from "the land of Egypt." We noticed earlier that some of the difficult areas of the Bible reflect the flawed culture of the day. It's worth, though, being especially attentive to the passages that *challenge* and *reject* the assumptions of their time.

In this new community, work was to be balanced with rest and refreshment, even for slaves (Exodus 20:8-11). Justice would be freely available to all, including foreigners and aliens (Exodus 23:6-9) and would be fair and impartial, not favoring the powerful and wealthy (Deuteronomy 16:18-20). Every member of the community would have an inalienable right to their share of the land, the farming land on which people living in an agricultural society depend for their sustenance and livelihood; land could be bought and sold, but periodically all land was to be returned to its original owners so that no family could be left destitute forever while others prospered on the back of their misfortune (Leviticus 25:8-55). Tithes were to be set aside from the produce of the land to provide for communal celebrations, and provision was to be at these celebrations for Levites (who owned no land), widows, aliens, orphans, and others whose poverty might otherwise exclude them (Deuteronomy 14:22-29). In these, and so many other ways, the community was to be quite distinct from those around, uniquely expressing the character of God's kingdom in concrete form.

Turning to the Gospels, though, we see a fascinating phenomenon. By the time of Jesus these radical innovations that rewrote the structures of society to offer greater freedom, equity, and justice had become a calcified status quo bolstering the power of the already powerful and entangling the day-to-day lives of the poorest and weakest. In response to this, some seemed to want to push against the provisions of the Hebrew covenant, arguing for a relaxation of its more arcane provisions; there had been furious arguments within Judaism in the centuries before Jesus' birth about the degree of accommodation that faithful Jews could make with the prevailing Greek culture. Others, in response, invested all their efforts in pressing for an ever more rigorous application of the covenant in all its tiniest details: the Pharisees were perhaps the leading proponents of this position.

Jesus steers a different course, and a surprising one. He boldly and decisively *innovates* the law. Over and over again he takes the provisions of the Hebrew covenant, roots out their inner spirit and purpose, and deftly reframes their application in people's lives. So we find the repeated refrain in the Sermon on the Mount: "You have heard that it was said ... but I say to you ..." (Matthew 5:21-48). Jesus defends his disciples for picking grain on the sabbath (Matthew 12:1-8) or seeking healing on the sabbath (Luke 13:10-17). He recasts the food laws to speak more about inner purity than the ritual cleanness of food (Mark 7:14-23) and infuriates the Pharisees by keeping company with unclean people (Mark 2:15-17). Jesus refused either to dispense with the law or allow people to become hopelessly entangled by it. Instead he reinterpreted it, offering a fresh perspective that had less to do with adherence to abstract divine principles and more to do with living a life of love in the presence of a loving heavenly Father.

THE POSSIBILITY OF CHANGE

Finally the Hebrew law envisioned a community of transformed people, those who had been set free from slavery—and not only from the literal slavery they had experienced in Egypt but also from the internal slavery to disordered and broken living that characterizes the human condition. Scripture dreams of a society of people able to live in new relationships with one another because each person has been renewed from within by the Spirit of God: hence the frequent refrain that the people are to "be holy, for I the LORD your God am holy" (Leviticus 19:2; see also Leviticus 11:44; 20:7).

The prophets, speaking and writing later in the history of Israel, were the ones who did most to keep alive this revolutionary vision of a changed society. Their lively and often fiery rhetoric continually reminded people of the value of the poor and outcast, the need for justice and equity in human relationships, the sacredness of seemingly secular life. God, they proclaimed, is interested in equality and well-being, in governance and economics, in the grit and dirt of politics and society. Listen again to the ringing words of Isaiah, adopted by Jesus to describe his own life and mission, which send shivers down the spine.

> The spirit of the Lord GOD is upon me,
>   because the LORD has anointed me;
> he has sent me to bring good news to the oppressed,
>   to bind up the brokenhearted,
> to proclaim liberty to the captives,
>   and release to the prisoners;
> to proclaim the year of the LORD's favor. (Isaiah 61:1-2)

The cadences of these biblical poets still echo down to our own day, recalled (for example) in the astonishing speech given by Martin Luther King Jr. at the Lincoln Memorial in 1963:

> I have a dream that one day this nation will rise up and live out the true meaning of its creed: "We hold these truths to be self-evident, that all men are created equal ..."

I have a dream that my four little children will one day live in a nation where they will not be judged by the color of their skin but by the content of their character.

I have a dream today! [...]

When we allow freedom ring, when we let it ring from every village and every hamlet, from every state and every city, we will be able to speed up that day when all of God's children, black men and white men, Jews and Gentiles, Protestants and Catholics, will be able to join hands and sing in the words of the old Negro spiritual:

Free at last! Free at last!

Thank God Almighty, we are free at last!

The law and prophets present us with a vision of a renewed people living in a loving community centered on God—God who called it into being, sustains its existence, and inhabits it intimately. The Hebrew Bible, for all its strangeness, is simply the first glimpse of the kingdom.

A KINGDOM IN CONFLICT

This, then, was the context and tradition within which Jesus offered a renewed invitation to all the people to experience life in loving community. It's a message with an inescapably social—and therefore political—dimension. And he was very clear that the coming of the kingdom represented a direct threat to the continuation of the prevailing social order, warning those with vested interests in the existing structures of society that they could quickly find themselves on a collision course with God's intervention in human affairs:

Blessed are you who are poor,
    for yours is the kingdom of God.
Blessed are you who are hungry now,
    for you will be filled.
Blessed are you who weep now,

for you will laugh. . . .

But woe to you who are rich,

　for you have received your consolation.

Woe to you who are full now,

　for you will be hungry.

Woe to you who are laughing now,

　for you will mourn and weep. (Luke 6:20-25)

As a result, Jesus taught that, even for his faithful followers, the pursuit of life in God's kingdom community would mean inevitable conflict with the existing order. "I am sending you out like sheep into the midst of wolves," he told his followers; "they will hand you over to councils and flog you in their synagogues; and you will be dragged before governors and kings because of me. . . . Do not think that I have come to bring peace to the earth; I have not come to bring peace, but a sword" (Matthew 10:16-18, 34). "I came to bring fire to the earth," he told them, "and how I wish it were already kindled!" (Luke 12:49). It is clear that Jesus saw God's coming kingdom as a tremendous gift for those who would readily receive it, especially those whose previously broken and painful lives would be utterly transformed by the renewing power of God's Spirit enabling them to flourish in a community of loving grace. But it would come as a disorienting shock to those who were already flourishing in the disordered, dog-eat-dog societies with which many of us are more familiar in our day-to-day lives.

This was certainly the case for Jesus himself. His message and actions antagonized all the leading power blocs in his first-century Palestinian society. He found himself repeatedly at odds with the Pharisees, the leading religious renewal movement in his day, and with the ruling Jerusalem elite of the Sadducees. He was closely watched with suspicion by the Galilean king Herod and his court, who eventually cooperated in his arrest and trial. And in the final week of his life, after having ridden into Jerusalem while the crowd acclaimed him as "Messiah" and "Son of David" (a royal—and therefore political—title), he found himself face to face with the implacable power of Rome in the person of Pontius Pilate. It's worth noting that Jesus was tried in the Jewish courts for a religious crime (claiming to be the Messiah) but executed by Roman soldiers for the political crime of sedition. After he was nailed to the cross, Matthew tells us, "over his head they put the charge against him, which read, 'This is Jesus, the King of the Jews'" (Matthew 27:37). The proclamation of the kingdom of God had crashed headlong into the powers of this present age.

The dream of God's loving community appeared to have foundered against the harsh realities of the "real" world. The earth shuddered, darkness drew in, and hope was laid in a cold stone tomb. Violence triumphed over mercy, force over gentleness, the assertion of naked power over the optimism of love. For three days the vision of the kingdom lay dead. For three days. And then everything changed.

THE KINGDOM
TODAY

To FOLLOW JESUS is to accept his call to participate in the gift of God's kingdom realized in our own time and place, and so to live as members of the God-soaked community of love. Accepting this call draws us into a new and alternative sociological and political reality, different from anything that already exists around us. Our present contexts, whether "thrones or dominions or rulers or powers" (Colossians 1:16), whether tyrannies or dictatorships or communes or democracies, may choose a more or less peaceful coexistence with the kingdom that is inevitably revealing itself in their midst. They may resist the kingdom with violence, embrace it with joy, or attempt to seduce and subvert it with charm. But they cannot replace it, nor co-opt it to their own ends, no matter how hard they may try. "My kingdom is not from this world" (John 18:36), Jesus told Pilate; it is not forged in palaces and parliaments. Any attempt to identify the kingdom with existing political alignments or parties, or with national institutions and interests, has a corrosive effect.

In the last resort all human powers, institutions, and ideologies have a tendency toward becoming what the German writer Karl Barth once described as *herrenlose Gewalten*: the deliberately ambiguous phrase can be translated either "lordless powers" (which are not accountable to God) or "stray powers" (which have lost their way). The proclamation of the kingdom challenges them, by explicitly naming the Lord they seek to deny, and offers them guidance, by showing the way toward an alternative model of community under God. Depending on the response, followers of Jesus who seek to participate in the life of the kingdom may find themselves either cooperating with the structures of their own society, fostering in them more of the character of the kingdom, or meeting bitter opposition and danger as their society forces them to make difficult choices and bear painful burdens. Peaceful coexistence may always be the more desirable option, but at times demonstrating love for those around us in our faithfulness to the kingdom vision can mean offering determined resistance to the inhuman governance under which we find ourselves.

PEOPLE OF PEACE

The first followers of Jesus understood this paradox of peaceful resistance from their own experience. At times, their relationship with the Roman authorities was amicable and cooperative. The apostle Paul once wrote to the community in Rome, living in the shadow of Caesar's palace and the Roman Senate:

> Let every person be subject to the governing authorities; for there is no authority except from God, and those authorities that exist have been instituted by God. Therefore whoever resists authority resists what God has appointed, and those who resist will incur judgment. (Romans 13:1-2)

Paul's letter to Rome was written a decade or so before the first major Roman persecution of Jesus' followers under the emperor Nero. Paul's readers, who were unlikely to have been in any position to question or challenge the expansionist and militaristic nature of the wider empire, would have experienced a daily life in the city that was largely secure, safe, well ordered, and appreciated by the majority of its residents. Rome was not the kingdom of God. But there was no obvious reason why those participating in the life of the kingdom might not do so while living peaceably and generously with the neighbors.

Paul, then, encourages *submission* and *peacemaking* within a wider society that is willing to accept the life of a kingdom-centered community in its midst. In this he echoes the guidance of the prophet Jeremiah to the Jewish exiles who found themselves resettled in Babylonia after the conquest of their nation and the destruction of Jerusalem. Despite the violence of that conquest, and the trauma of their resettlement far from their homeland, the exiles found themselves accommodated and tolerated within the city of Babylon. It wasn't an easy or comfortable arrangement, and they yearned both for vengeance on their captors and for restoration to their shattered homeland. It might have seemed natural and right for them to rage against the Babylonians, acting openly or subversively against their interests, and actively seek their downfall. But Jeremiah steers them in a very different direction:

> Thus says the LORD of hosts, the God of Israel, to all the exiles whom I have sent into exile from Jerusalem to Babylon: Build houses and live in them; plant gardens and eat what they produce. Take wives and have sons and daughters; take wives for your sons, and give your daughters in marriage, that they may bear sons and daughters; multiply there, and do not decrease. But seek the welfare of the city where I have sent you into exile, and pray to the LORD on its behalf, for in its welfare you will find your welfare. (Jeremiah 29:4-7)

There is an echo of this approach in the teaching of Jesus to his followers before he sent them out into the towns and villages to share the news about the kingdom: "Whatever house you enter, first say, 'Peace to this house!' And if anyone is there who shares in peace, your peace will rest on that person; but if not, it will return to you. Remain in the same house, eating and drinking whatever they provide" (Luke 10:5-7).

In some ways, acting the part of the firebrand prophet is easy and gratifying. There can be a perverse pleasure in tearing down rather than building up; watch any toddler at work on a brick model! It is, after all, usually easier to identify a problem than to fix it, simpler to lambast those in leadership than it is to lead. But if the kingdom of God is about participation in a God-soaked loving community, we must always be more ready to live in love with others than to confront them. Wherever we find people of peace, we should seek to work alongside them, settle among them, share our peace with them, receive the gift of their hospitality, and be ready to extend ours. Wherever possible, we "seek the welfare of the city" in ways that are positive, contributory, and participative.

STANDING FIRM

However, the early community of Jesus-followers was unable to maintain their peaceful existence within the Roman Empire indefinitely. Rome was founded on a polytheistic faith that was content to incorporate other nations' gods into its pantheon but reluctant to give space to spiritual communities who resisted this process of assimilation. The Jewish people had experienced an uneasy relationship with Rome for many years, as periods of calm fluctuated with times of tension. The crunch, for both Jews and the early Jesus-followers, came as the emperors began to proclaim themselves as living divinities and include themselves in the civic pantheon. This shift in relationship was accompanied by an instability in the psychological health of the emperors (this was the era of such figures as Caligula and Nero) who were given to violent persecution of those who resisted their increasingly despotic rule. As a result, Paul's policy of remaining "subject to the governing authorities" became unsustainable.

When an entire society implacably resists loving community, *dissent* is often the only loving response. If the prophetic voices of the Hebrew Bible have anything to teach us, it must be that justice cannot be wrought from unjust laws, that peace is never forged from violence, and that extorted wealth corrodes the lives of rich and poor alike. When the moral foundation of our social lives crumbles, we cannot sit idly by; the well-being of the outcasts, the beggars, the minorities, the persecuted, and the powerless is the well-being of all.

Those whose lives are shaped by the vision of God's kingdom will speak out and will act—with hope, with courage, and above all with love. At times the right place for the follower of Jesus is in the parliaments and senates, in the debating chambers and courtrooms, shaping the laws that shape society. At times it is among the poor and underprivileged, giving dignity to their lives and stories, alleviating their need. At times, though, it is in the streets: marching, confronting, challenging the "the cosmic powers of this present darkness" (Ephesians 6:12) and announcing the alternative of the kingdom.

Such dissent is dangerous. For those seeking life in the kingdom, we always accept the danger entirely on ourselves. We may be called to walk in the footsteps of Jesus, who was arrested, falsely accused, unjustly imprisoned, publicly humiliated, and painfully executed. "A disciple is not above the teacher," Jesus warned, "nor a slave above the master. . . . If they called the master of the house Beelzebul [a name of the devil], how much more will they malign those of his household!" (Matthew 10:24-25). The earliest followers of Jesus bore a brutal cost for their dissent. The historian Tacitus records that during the reign of Nero they were arrested and tortured to death for sport: trussed up in animal hides to be savaged by dogs, burned alive to provide torchlight for evening parties in the imperial gardens, or crucified in imitation of their Master. In more recent times, Martin Luther King Jr. challenged the racist foundations of his contemporary American society with a vision of equality and loving community drawn directly from the teaching of Jesus in the Gospels; he also paid in blood for speaking out.

But we dare not return violence with violence, even in the name of justice. There are those in every age who wrestle, in good conscience, with this question: Can it never be right to take up arms against an oppressive government, to defend the weak and powerless with power and strength, to overthrow with force an iniquitous regime? The issues are complex and the questions asked in the face of great pain and suffering. All the kingdom community can do is point to the Gospels and reply: this is not the way of Jesus. "All who take the sword will perish by the sword" (Matthew 26:52), he once said, holding back his disciples as they sought to protect him from unjust arrest. "Do not resist an evildoer," he said on another occasion; "but if anyone strikes you on the right cheek, turn the other also" (Matthew 5:39).

This is the politics of Jesus. A politics of engagement and creative coexistence. A politics sometimes of dissent and resistance. But always the politics of the kingdom, and therefore always a politics of love.

OVER TO YOU

Scripture and Reflection

In THIS FINAL SECTION we've explored the political significance of Jesus' life and teaching, and how that was received and understood by his contemporaries. We looked at the way the Hebrew Scriptures sought to envision a social and communal life quite unlike any other in the ancient world: a community modeled on God's kingdom vision. We saw how the prophets continued to express that vision whenever it was compromised or resisted by their national leaders and institutions, creating a school of thought on which Jesus built his own public life and teaching. And we considered the ways in which followers of Jesus should be engaged with their own political context—sometimes cooperatively and sometimes with vigorous resistance.

The following are another set of readings and questions to aid you in your own reflection and thinking about these issues. Once again, you may want to spend time with these on a day-by-day basis over the coming week. Alternatively, you might find it more useful to select those passages and ideas that are most relevant to you at the present moment.

- *Deuteronomy 30:11-20*

    What seems most life-giving about the social and political life described in the opening books of the Bible? What do you find most difficult?

- *Exodus 20:1-17*

    In what ways could the Ten Commandments form a solid basis for national life? What would be difficult to live out in practice? What is *not* expressed in these words that would be essential or desirable?

- *Jeremiah 1:4-10*

    What do you find most compelling or inspiring about the Hebrew prophets? What do you find least attractive?

- *Luke 22:24-30*

    What do you think good political and social leadership looks like? How can those in positions of leadership continue to live as servants of others?

- *Jeremiah 29:4-7*

    Where do you think you should be engaged in submission and peacemaking with the society you live in? What could that look like in practice?

- *Acts 4:13-26*

    Where do you think you should be engaged in resistance and dissent against the society you live in? What could that look like in practice?

- *Revelation 6:9-11*

    What would you be willing to give your life for? How can we maintain the courage to dissent in the face of violent persecution?

EPILOGUE

IMAGINE THE DAY *BEFORE* YOUR DEATH.

Imagine yourself about to leave this world, to say farewell to all its beauty and sorrow, its glory and darkness. You've become deeply aware that over this world the Holy Spirit will continue to brood, that God will continue to call forth purpose, life, joy, grace, and love every single day. You've seen it happen.

You remember all the ways that life in this world has offered you experiences of God and of his love. The gift of your own life, utterly unasked and unearned but given anyway. The gift of other people, some of whom you have learned to love very deeply. The gift of community, which held you in dark times and sang with joy when you were rejoicing. The strange but precious gifts of struggle, sadness, and loss.

You think back over your mistakes. Of course there are regrets, perhaps many. But that makes you conscious also of the mercy and forgiveness you experienced from God and from those who loved you.

So close to the end, you're finally able to see clearly what really mattered. Perhaps not, as it turns out, your wealth, your reputation, your sense of achievement, your possessions, your career—all those things you were so attentive to over the years. Instead, you see that it was always about people and relationships. About love, kindness, gentleness, grace, compassion, friendship. The earth you walked on and took so often for granted mattered: its trees and clouds, its winding lanes and wide open fields, its mountains and oceans now seem so unbearably glorious. And God. God mattered, still matters. God shaped this world, filled this world, breathed life into this world. Everything around you had always been joyfully crying out his name, if only you'd stopped to listen. And your friendship with God, you realize, always meant so much too.

From the beginning, God had been creating a community of loving people in which he would dwell. And he invited you to share in the life of that community, to open your poor disordered heart to the healing touch of his Spirit so you could be transformed into a loving, Christlike member of his family. And this, in the end, was maybe what mattered most of all.

Imagine how you might have lived if you'd simply realized this sooner! How your attitude to work, family, community, play, possessions, food, strangers, art, and music—your attitude to everything—might have been so different. Imagine how you might have lived, if you'd simply understood that the kingdom was real, the most real thing in your life.

Would your relationships have been any different? How might you have lived differently among your family, your community, the folks in your neighborhood? Everything that seemed so important to you—being right, being in charge, being respected, being admired—might you have let that go a little? These people suddenly seem like an astonishingly valuable gift about to slip from your fingers. How could it all have been different?

What about the stuff that filled the hours of your day? Did you, after all, find meaning and purpose in it? Were you able to be creative, nurturing, expressive, helpful, joyful, at least from time to time? Did you find *satisfaction* and *fulfillment* in your life? Where did that happen—and where did it not? Were there other choices you could have made or would have made?

Would you have found it so difficult to forgive if you'd known what you know now: that life is fleeting and relationships are so precious, that everyone else is as frail, troubled, and damaged as you are, that life is difficult enough without us making it harder for one another? Imagine how patient, generous, gracious, and merciful you could have been if you'd understood how much those people really mattered to God and to you.

Imagine, as these questions turn around in your mind, that one more floats to the surface: Why was I so afraid? Why did I worry so much about my job, my reputation, my security, my influence, my legacy, my responsibilities? Why was it so hard to trust? The swirling cosmos came into being at a single word from God, without any help from me. Why didn't I believe God could hold it together without my anxious intervention? Might it really be, as an ancient mystic one said, that all shall be well, and all shall be well, and all manner of things shall be well?

Imagine this moment—as everything superfluous and insubstantial about this life falls away, and all that really matters comes into sharp focus, and at last you are able to hear the ravishing delight of the song of God being sung over this world, over your life, over *you*.

Now imagine one more thing. Imagine this is not the day before you die. Instead, it is simply *today*. Another ordinary day in this extraordinary life. Imagine that you still have time: time to explore, to learn, to grow, to change, to live.

What might it look like for you today—this wild, beautiful, magnificent God-soaked life?

TAKING PART

So how do we live a God-soaked life?

1. We accept Jesus' invitation to participate in God's community of love.

2. We are seeking the renewal of our hearts so we can love as Christ loves.

3. We are fearlessly honest about our weaknesses, failures, and limits.

4. We long to experience God in silence, prayer, and Scripture.

5. We nurture an awareness of God in everyday life.

6. We share life together with love, grace, mercy, and reconciliation.

7. We have the hope and courage to challenge the "lordless powers."

Who are "we"? Simply you and me, held together by the pages of this book. And all those others who read it and share the same desire and commitment. And every other person longing for a God-soaked life who embraces this same covenant without even being conscious of it.

We follow Jesus. The truth is, we don't always fully understand his teaching, and we don't always succeed in emulating his life. Sometimes we disagree among ourselves about what following him means. We're frail and human and we make mistakes. Still, as best we can, we follow Jesus. That's enough.

Wherever we find communities of people pursuing this God-soaked life, we throw our lot in with them enthusiastically. We have a lot to learn from each other. We are all human and therefore prone to making mistakes. We understand that about each other. We try to be as forgiving of these communities as they need to be of us. We're all getting it wrong a lot of the time, and that's fine. After all, in the end it's not about us anyway.

We are a movement, of a sort. Because we have a destination, of a sort. We're not trying to move other people, though; we're trying to move ourselves. And oddly, our destination is right where we are. We know we couldn't be nearer to heaven than we are right now, because we're already living in a magnificent world drenched with the presence of God. But we seem to have trouble living there. Our thoughts are often in the past or future. Our attention is often elsewhere. We're slowly learning to deal with that, to recognize that God is here in this place, among these people.

We don't have a motto, but if we did it might be *revelatur ambulando*: "it's revealed as we walk." We don't have all the answers right now, but by following in the footsteps of Jesus we find more and more clarity—along with plenty more questions. Another, looser translation might be: "we're making this up as we go along." That's probably fair too.

If you want to be part of the movement, you already are. Feel free to tell people you're one of us, although frankly they probably already know. Desire is like that; it's hard to hide.

ACKNOWLEDGMENTS

Sɪɴᴄᴇ ɪᴛ sʜᴏᴜʟᴅ ʙᴇ ɪᴍᴍᴇᴅɪᴀᴛᴇʟʏ ᴏʙᴠɪᴏᴜs, let me say this first: I'm perfectly capable of making all my own mistakes and don't appear to need any help in that department. Every error, inadequacy, wrong turn, or poor piece of phrasing has been lovingly crafted by me and me alone. I won't let anyone else take credit for it.

That said, if there's good in this book it's largely come from the wide and diverse community of people around me who have helped me, over many years now, to become a better lover of Jesus. It'd be nice to thank just a few of them.

A lot of the thinking in this book started coming together while I was living in Colorado and working as president of Renovaré USA, and there are conversations that began during that time which I've had the privilege to continue over the years since. Gary Moon, Mickey Cox, Lacy Borgo: I'm particularly looking at you. And because even after I moved back to the United Kingdom they kept bringing me back to teach on the Renovaré Institute for Christian Spiritual Formation, I had the chance to learn from and (occasionally) spar with the students from a variety of cohorts. Thanks to you all! I know we didn't always agree, but that's fine. You knew how to think well, pray hard, and challenge graciously. You're magnificent.

My colleagues here in Leicester now have been equally wonderful, both creating space for me to write and encouraging my thinking. I'm tremendously grateful to Alison Christian, David and Helen Newman,

Cathy Davies, Hazel Aucken, and the rest of the folks here at Launde Abbey. You might recognize tiny snippets of our conversations all over this book. You helped me write it, even when you didn't know you were doing it.

Likewise my colleagues at the Mission and Ministry Department in the Diocese of Leicester have been a fantastic support. It would be wrong to single out individuals, but I'll do it anyway. Jonathan Dowman: thanks for the teaching invitation that first spurred the creation of this book. And Stuart Burns, Barry Hill, Mads Morgan, Nicky McGinty, and the rest of the crew: I love you all, and I'm naming those guys especially because doing DLP with you changed my life and, as you know, made this book possible. Thanks!

In my work as Spirituality Adviser to the Diocese of Leicester I work with a huge number of churches, Anglican and other, across the English east Midlands, but one in particular has provided me with a spiritual home and has let me explore these ideas with the congregation, even though my outlook is often very different from theirs and we've had some very gracious, friendly, but also sparky debates. St. Luke's in Thurnby: you've made this book possible, and you'll recognize much of what I've written here. Particular thanks to Jon Barrett for your friendship and for being so hospitable to your weird monk!

The good folks at InterVarsity Press have been as brilliant as ever, especially the infinitely patient and wise Cindy Bunch. If this reads like a real book rather than a loose collection of thoughts and ideas, just know this: Cindy made that happen.

And then, of course, there's my family. I sometimes feel as if writing a book is like bringing a new child into the house, a demanding and petulant infant who sucks all the time and energy out of you. You become preoccupied and neglectful. You're up at odd hours fussing over the precious little thing. And your family, apparently, just accepts this massive intrusion, suffers your absences and distractions with Stoic calm, and patiently waits to get you back again. So: thanks to you guys, Benedict, Bethan, Francis, and Gregory. And especially to my wonderful and magnificent Sally. I love you all, and clearly you guys love me a great deal in return.

There are others, of course. I hope you know who you all are, and also that I'm really grateful. I'd be happy to acknowledge you, effusively and by name, in any future books. All I ask in return is ice cream. Everyone has their price, and that's mine.

NOTES

1: THE INVITATION

18-19 *young deacon called Lawrence*: I'm recounting (and paraphrasing) this story about Lawrence from memory. Ambrose of Milan wrote an early life of Lawrence describing this incident; a more lively account can be found in the early fifth-century "Hymn in Honor of the Blessed Martyr Lawrence," by Prudentius. An English translation can be found in M. Clement Eagan, *The Poems of Prudentius* (Washington, DC: Catholic University of America Press, 1962).

22 *Behold God beholding you*: Anthony de Mello, quoted in Michael Harter, *Hearts on Fire: Praying with Jesuits* (St. Louis: Institute of Jesuit Sources, 1993), 9.

3: FEARLESS HONESTY

73-74 *Egyptian desert monk Anthony the Great*: Anthony the Great, *The Sayings of the Desert Fathers*, trans. Benedicta Ward (Collegeville, MN: Cistercian Publications, 1975), 6.

4: CLOSE TO THE FATHER'S HEART

87 *survey conducted in the United Kingdom*: David Hay and Kate Hunt, "Understanding the Spirituality of People Who Don't Go to Church," University of Nottingham, 2000, 9, www.churchofscotland.org .uk/__data/assets/.../understanding_spirituality_report.pdf.

88 *When I try to raise my thoughts to Heaven*: Mother Teresa, *Mother Teresa: Come Be My Light*, ed. Brian Kolodiejchuk (New York: Doubleday Religion, 2008), 187.

96 *Describe the aroma of coffee*: Ludwig Wittgenstein, quoted in H. O. Mounce, "The Aroma of Coffee," *Philosophy* 64, no. 248 (April 1989): 159.

5: GOD IN EVERYDAY LIFE

105 *Glory be to God for dappled things*: Gerard Manley Hopkins, "Pied Beauty" (1877), in *Poems and Prose*, ed. W. H. Gardner (New York: Penguin, 1985), 30-31.

107 *I saw the inscape*: Gerard Manley Hopkins, *The Collected Works of Gerard Manley Hopkins*, ed. Lesley Higgins (New York: Oxford University Press, 2015), 3:544.

What you look at hard: Ibid., 504.

The world is charged with the grandeur of God: Gerard Manley Hopkins, "Gods' Grandeur" (1877), in Gardner, *Poems and Prose*, 27.

110 *One day in winter while he was looking*: Joseph de Beaufort, quoted in Brother Lawrence, *The Practice of the Presence of God: Critical Edition*, trans. Salvatore Sciurba (Washington, DC: ICS Publications, 1994), 89.

120 *an outward and visible sign*: This is the definition used in the 1662 Book of Common Prayer of the Church of England. It echoes words used by Augustine of Hippo in the early fifth century: "the signs of divine things are, it is true, things visible, but . . . invisible things themselves are also honored in them." Augustine, *On the Catechising of the Uninstructed* 26.50, trans. S. D. F. Salmond, in Nicene and Post-Nicene Fathers 3, ed. Philip Schaff (Peabody, MA: Hendrickson, 1994), 312.

123 *To see a World in a Grain of Sand*: William Blake, "Auguries of Innocence" (1863), in *The Complete Poetry and Prose of William Blake*, ed. David V. Erdman (New York: Anchor, 1988), 493.

6: CREATING COMMUNITY

131-32 *an unspeakable gift of God for the lonely individual*: Dietrich Bonhoeffer, *Life Together* (Norwich, UK: SCM Press, 1954), 10.

137 *Show, if you can, why you should not obey*: The speaker is quoted in David J. Bosch, *Transforming Mission* (Maryknoll, NY: Orbis Books, 1991), 341.

All mission flows from God's sovereignty: Abraham Kuyper, quoted in ibid., 349.

141   *The church exists by mission*: Emil Brunner, *The Word and the World* (Norwich, UK: SCM Press, 1931), 108.

7: THE POLITICS OF LOVE

157   *symptomatic of a silliness*: George F. Will, "Jesus as Che," *Washington Post*, February 14, 1999, www.washingtonpost.com/archive/opinions /1999/02/14/jesus-as-che/cea4676b-483d-4133-a68c-603698d6e67a /?utm_term=.b75cb5cbcb92.

164   *It wasn't until 1938 that the teachings*: Robert Smith, quoted in *The Co-Founders of Alcoholics Anonymous: Biographical Sketches and Their Last Major Talks* (New York: Alcoholics Anonymous World Services, 1975), 14.

170   *Karl Barth once described as* herrenlose Gewalten: Karl Barth, "The Christian Life," in *Church Dogmatics* IV.4 (Grand Rapids: Eerdmans, 1981), 213.